ROTARY CUTTING
REVOLUTION

NEW ONE-STEP CUTTING, 8 QUILT BLOCKS

ANITA GROSSMAN SOLOMON

C&T PUBLISHING

Text and Artwork copyright © 2010 by Anita Grossman Solomon

Artwork copyright © 2010 by C&T Publishing, Inc.

Publisher: Amy Marson

Creative Director: Gailen Runge

Acquisitions Editor: Susanne Woods

Editor: Liz Aneloski

Technical Editors: Sandy Peterson and Carolyn Aune

Copyeditor/Proofreader: Wordfirm Inc.

Cover/Book Designer: Kristen Yenche

Production Coordinator: Zinnia Heinzmann

Production Editor: Alice Mace Nakanishi

Illustrator: Aliza Shalit

Photography by Christina Carty-Francis and Diane Pedersen of C&T Publishing, Inc., unless otherwise noted.

Published by C&T Publishing, Inc., P.O. Box 1456, Lafayette, CA 94549

Library of Congress Cataloging-in-Publication Data

Solomon, Anita Grossman, 1954-

  Rotary cutting revolution : new one-step cutting, 8 quilt blocks / Anita Grossman Solomon.

    p. cm.

  Includes index.

  ISBN 978-1-57120-829-3

  1. Patchwork. 2. Quilting. 3. Rotary cutting. I. Title.

  TT835.S652134 2010

  746.46--dc22

                                    2009034772

Printed in China

10 9 8 7 6 5 4 3 2 1

CONTENTS

 DEDICATION

For HHS, the love of my life, the man of my dreams.

 ACKNOWLEDGMENTS

This book was lovingly encouraged by Horace H. Solomon and brought to fruition by this virtual village of friends, each one of whom is deserving of my sincere gratitude:

Liz Aneloski • Patricia Spergel Bauman • John Bellamy • Constance Benson • BJ Berti • Denise Bradley • Alexandra Lee Brovenick • Laura Yellen Catlan • Guy Clark • Emily Cohen • Judy Hoffman Corwin • Betty A. Davis • Ruth Brown and the Riverbank State Park Cultural Department • Margaret Marcy Emerson • Renée Kane Fields • Carol Goossens' • Jan Grigsby • Dorothea Hahn • Georgette Hasiotis • John Heisch • Jeremy Hofstetter • Mary Ellen Hopkins • Susan Liimatta Horn • Laurel Horton • Roberta Horton • Sylvia Hughes • Cathy Izzo and Dale Riehl of The City Quilter in New York • Frances Jackson • Adam Jaffe • Claudia Jaffe • Miriam Janove • Susan Kaletsky • Susan Knaster • Anna Krassy • Suzanne F. W. Lemakis • Roger LeMoine • Mary Mashuta • Melanie Matte • Ethel McCall • Penny McMorris • Harrison Morgan • Olga Norville • Gael O'Donnell • Diane Pedersen • Marcella Peek • Sandy Peterson • Lois Podolny • Ellen A. Quinn • Nancy Rabatin • Sarah Rhinelander • Dawn Rhodes • Gailen Runge • Eric Runge • Jake Runge • Kennedy Runge • Didi Schiller • Michele Shatz • Julie Silber • Phyllis Spalla • Kathryn Squire • Robin Strauss • Darra Williamson • Sara Woodward • Leslie Zemsky

Janice E. Petre of Janice Petre's House of Quilting in Sinking Spring, Pennsylvania, is a treasure who has collaborated with me since my first book, as has Susan Stauber, whose generosity and wit I continue to benefit from.

The following companies and representatives were generous in providing their time and products:

Gail Kessler, Andover Fabrics, New York, New York

Jeanne C. Delpit, Bernina of America, Aurora, Illinois

The Electric Quilt Company, Bowling Green, Ohio

Tracy Whitlock, Fairfield Processing Corp., Danbury, Connecticut

The International Quilt Study Center, Lincoln, Nebraska

Robert Kaufman Fabrics, Los Angeles, California

Lisa Shepard Stewart, Marcus Fabrics, New York, New York

Anne Scott, editor, *New Zealand Quilter,* Wellington, New Zealand

LaRonda S. Caldwell and Gwen Edwards, Prym Consumer, Spartanburg, South Carolina

Timeless Treasures Fabrics, New York, New York

ABOUT THIS BOOK

This collection of Make It Simpler Cutting Lines blocks introduces a quick, new, one-step way to cut your fabric pieces.

Starched, stacked, and uniformly trimmed squares are precisely cut into pieces in one step, without wasted fabric. No more cutting strips, then cutting strips into squares and rectangles, and cutting again into triangles.

Stacked, trimmed squares

One-step cutting

Two stacked and cut squares of fabric = two quilt blocks

THE BLOCKS

With these efficient construction shortcuts and no-waste methods, each block offers a lot of bang for the fabric buck. A Make It Simpler Block Cutting Chart (page 108) summarizes block measurements from start to finish.

No Patience Block

The Square Cut method produces four rectangles and a square from four rotary cuts. The construction method saves steps and preserves a directional fabric's orientation.

CUTTING GUIDES

Trimming and cutting is done in one continuous operation, sometimes through cutting patterns, which resemble line drawings of quilt blocks but with seam allowances included. A photocopied pattern is centered on a stack of fabric squares. Rotary cuts made through the pattern lines produce pieces for blocks, without measuring. For example, the 64 trapezoids and triangles needed for 2 Pineapple blocks are cut to shape with only 14 rotary cuts!

GLUE

Either a fabric or repositionable gluestick is used to lightly secure cutting patterns to fabric. Gluing to the wrong side of the fabric is an option.

GUIDELINES

Square acrylic cutting rulers are used to true up finished blocks. Markings made with a permanent felt-tip pen on the unmarked side of the ruler can be wiped clean with rubbing alcohol or nail polish remover.

Xcentric Block

Two identical squares of stripe fabric are sewn and cut to create blocks ordinarily made by cutting and sewing triangles and matching stripes. Large or small, a pair of blocks takes only four seams.

Anita's Arrowhead Block

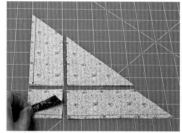

Its ten subunits are sewn with only two contiguous seams and *then* cut with three simple strokes. Astonishingly, four of these subunits are asymmetrical pairs.

Old Italian Block

This block is made from nine unpieced subunits cut in four strokes, using rotary mat gridlines as guides. A feature of the cutting plan is the sublime background and foreground effect that appears with printed fabric.

SUPPLY LIST

A list of supplies can be found at the end of this book (page 109). I prefer to use rulers as cutting templates, so several sizes are listed but are optional. One 12½" square ruler is sufficient for all cutting.

BLOCK CUTTING CHART

The Block Cutting Chart (page 108) consolidates cutting information. Keep a photocopy of it in your cutting area for reference.

FABRIC REQUIREMENTS

One square of fabric is needed per block; 100 quilt blocks use 100 squares of fabric. It's easy to estimate yardage requirements by counting the number of fabric squares. Anita's Arrowhead needs two 8" squares of fabric for each block; and the Self-Mitered Log Cabin, a fabric lover's playground, uses many strips instead of squares. Standard yardage and rotary ruler sizes were considered in determining block sizes.

No-Waste Windmill Block

  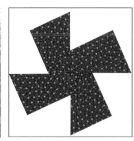

Four identical, non-square subunits are cut in two rotary strokes using a cutting pattern—no measuring. The block, made slightly oversize, is accurately squared because the cutting pattern doubles as a true-up guide. There are no corners or points to match when sewing the blocks together. An alternative paperless option for cutting is also presented.

Square-on-Point Block

  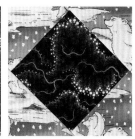

Following a cutting pattern, four triangles and an on-point square (none of which have lost their motif orientation) are cut from an oversize square. Optionally and miraculously, the block can be top foundation pieced onto a cutting pattern.

Pineapple Block

Not only are the needed 64 trapezoids and triangles created with only 14 rotary cuts, but in addition, surprising quilt layouts are made possible by slicing the blocks in unexpected ways to create setting pieces.

Self-Mitered Log Cabin Block

Without pins or peeking, 1½″ strips of fabric meet to form precisely mitered intersections.

PREFACE

by Laurel Horton

Laurel Horton has been making quilts and researching quiltmaking traditions since 1975. Her award-winning book Mary Black's Family Quilts: Memory and Meaning in Everyday Life *examines the quilts of one South Carolina family through the generations, showing how women used quilts to reinforce family connections. Laurel continues to make quilts for friends, family, and her own enjoyment. She has taught string patchwork at the John C. Campbell Folk School in Brasstown, North Carolina, since 1990, introducing this technique to hundreds of students.*

Self-Mitered Log Cabin, made by author; quilted by Janice E. Petre,
Sinking Spring, Pennsylvania; 2002–2008, 69″ × 81″

The visual beauty of quilts is often enhanced by the rich effects, afforded by the juxtaposition of light and dark fabrics. The Log Cabin design emerged in the mid-nineteenth century and quickly became a favorite among quiltmakers, who exploited the almost endless possibilities and created numerous variations. Even a lot of nonquilters can recognize the pattern and identify it by name.

Quiltmakers of the late nineteenth century enjoyed access to an abundance of printed cotton fabrics produced in New England factories. Fabric-buying habits shifted as women purchased small amounts of a larger number of fabrics, rather than whole bolts of just a few. Women expressed their delight in this abundance and variety in patchwork, and they particularly recognized the great potential of the Log Cabin design to perform individual acts of striking

beauty and visual distinction. Many of these stunning examples result from the way the vertical and horizontal orientation of the fabric strips is overshadowed by the diagonal counterpoint created by light and dark fabrics.

Countless quiltmakers through the years have enjoyed the process of dividing their fabrics into piles of lights and darks, then sewing the strips together by hand or by machine, either using a fabric foundation or not, starting in the center and building outward until the square is big enough. The maker might take passing pleasure in the way particular squares seem to develop personality, but the real delight comes in laying out the modules and seeing for the first time the emergence of the dark and light diagonals. At that moment, the maker becomes aware that the quilt is becoming something more than the sum of its parts.

Of the various arrangements of Log Cabin blocks that have merited names of their own, the barn raising variation probably holds the record for eliciting the most stunned silences, jaw drops, and exhalations of awe. Depending on the colors and patterning of the fabrics, the concentric diamond of a Barn Raising Log Cabin can produce a surface of sophisticated graphic starkness, a vibrant ethereal shimmer, or the illusion of dark outlines suspended in front of an illuminated haze.

Cynics have suggested that some of these punchy visual effects resulted accidentally, from unplanned combinations of random remnants. Or, even less charitably, that the maker, lacking knowledge of the Op Art movement, was incapable of seeing her quilt in the same way as our more sophisticated modern eyes. What snobbery! It's true that quiltmakers of the past lacked the gallery walls and personal photography that allow us to step back and encompass the visual complexity of a quilt. But nearly every quiltmaker had access to a clothesline.

What Anita Grossman Solomon offers with her Self-Mitered Log Cabin process is as much a product of nineteenth-century quilt aesthetics as it is of twenty-first-century technology. Her examples retain the visual illusion and the breath-catching sensation of midair suspension with the best of the historic Barn Raising Log Cabins. They even retain that delicious internal contradiction of diagonal forms superimposed over horizontal and vertical elements. But following the lead of generations of quiltmakers who ask, "What if?" Anita takes hold of tradition and plays around with it.

The tools and toys available to today's quiltmakers include not only fabric, scissors, paper, and sewing machines, but also gluesticks, rotary cutters, and photocopiers. But the primary innovation of Anita's interpretation is not dependent on new technology; it is merely an extension of the traditional quiltmaker's impulse. Instead of separating her fabrics into two piles, she arranges them into a series of light-to-dark gradations. In theory, one could use this principle while constructing a standard Log Cabin block, but I suspect that would turn an enjoyable experience into an unnecessarily fussy one.

Not only does this Make It Simpler technique build on a traditional Log Cabin footing, but it also rests on the much more recent process of machine piecing on paper

Reality Check, by author, 1997, 37″ square

foundations. The individual printed-paper blocks that we saw as the latest thing almost two decades ago have found a place in the canon of options available to quiltmakers. And like earlier innovations that became traditional, paper-foundation piecing has evolved through multiple interpretations and variations.

Quiltmakers often speak of traditional and contemporary quiltmaking as if these were two different entities. Or we think about these terms as describing two ends of a single spectrum. The reality is probably more complicated than that and much more interesting. Some fabric artists create expressionistic surfaces, using splashes of color in asymmetrical disorder; yet they sew by hand. Others use new technology to perform geometric acrobatics, producing the familiar look and feel of historic quilts completely by machine. One quiltmaker carefully purchases the fat quarters to give her daughter's wedding quilt a "scrap look," while another scavenges fabric from thrift stores to make wallhangings sold in a gallery. Who's to say that one is traditional and the other contemporary? Ultimately, such labels become a lot less important than the fact that each of these quilts is the result of an individual process that involves mental, emotional, and physical components. The finished quilt may or may not look like others, but the inner experience of the maker can never be replicated.

Pineapple quilt, of Iowa origin, collection of author, circa 1880, 75″ × 73″

American quiltmaking includes many different interpretations of a Pineapple. These include a family of appliqué designs; a pieced, four-pointed star with sawtooth edges, also known as Pine Burr or Pine Cone (see *Encyclopedia of Pieced Quilt Patterns,* compiled by Barbara Brackman; American Quilter's Society); and the elaborated Log Cabin featured in this publication. Like the original Log Cabin, this Pineapple was traditionally sewn on a foundation of fabric squares. Many surviving examples from the mid-nineteenth century are flat-quilted; that is, they are finished without a middle layer of batting.

These earliest Pineapple quilts were typically constructed from silk or wool, indicating that they were made by women who could afford the time and materials to make decorative needlework. Later, as inexpensive cotton prints became available to a wider segment of the population,

more quiltmakers explored the design properties of these versatile new fabrics. The Pineapple variation of the Log Cabin remained one of the popular patterns for cotton patchwork during the late nineteenth century.

Sources of information about the origins and early development of nineteenth-century patchwork patterns are almost nonexistent. But in the case of the Pineapple, we can imagine one possible scenario leading to its emergence. A hypothetical quiltmaker is piecing her Log Cabin blocks, trying out this brand-new technique, just as her fashionable friends are all doing. She is hand-sewing small strips of silk onto a square of cotton. She completes a seam and finger-presses the strip into place, and only then does she notice that one end of the strip doesn't extend all the way to where the next seam would cover it. She hates it when that happens!

Scrappy Pineapple, made by author; quilted by Janice E. Petre, Sinking Spring, Pennsylvania; 2007, 74″ square

She stares at the unfinished block, her frustration mounting. Silk is such a slippery fabric. She wishes she had never started this project, but she's committed now, having cut this fine fabric into all those little pieces. If she leaves in the imperfect strip, her friends will notice, but she really doesn't want to take it out. As she sits there, conflicting desires and motivations filling her head, she suddenly has an idea. She takes another strip of silk, and she places it diagonally across the corner of the patchwork, covering the offending strip. She likes the way it looks. She smiles and sews it into place. Emboldened and inspired, she does the same with all the corners, and then, with the remaining blocks. She can hardly wait to show her friends.

We don't know if this is the way it happened. It's possible that our mid-nineteenth-century quiltmaker simply decided to try something different. Young women from well-to-do families typically studied geometry in private or public schools during this period.

Historic Pineapple quilts demonstrate a range of design options. Some makers interpreted the pattern in two colors, most often in red and white, resulting in a stark, high-contrast graphic surface. But many others took the opportunity to mingle a variety of different colors, textures, and patterning while maintaining a light/dark contrast.

Anita's quilt (above) replicates the rich, kaleidoscopic complexity of this traditional style. From a distance, the vision of those pale, prickly circles around the dark sprouting squares might cause a viewer to stop and wonder when it was made. Walking closer, the viewer would recognize contemporary fabrics and smile at the maker's reference to quilts of the past. This viewer might also marvel that a modern quiltmaker would go through the trouble of

Log Cabin pattern, Pennsylvania, circa 1880–1900, 68½″ × 69½″
International Quilt Study Center & Museum, University of Nebraska–Lincoln, 1997.007.0923

piecing such an intricate design, not realizing that the maker followed a newfangled process to achieve a traditional result.

Some nineteenth-century quiltmakers used the Pineapple block as a beginning point for individual experimentation. At first glance, some of these quilts may be dismissed as utilitarian scrap quilts, but a closer look sometimes reveals something more.

The unknown maker of one quilt (above) wasn't interested in creating a secondary, overall pattern. Instead, she explored the various ways she could combine and juxtapose colors, highlighting selected parts of the design, producing a quilt in which no two blocks are alike. What a playful approach! The maker maintained a modicum of order in her quilt by placing an orange square in the center of each block and by selecting a neutral gray—actually several different gray fabrics—for the background.

Five of the blocks were pieced with wings of a single, dark/medium solid color alternating with the receding, mottled gray. A sixth block catches the eye with wings of solid white. Did the quiltmaker start by making these two-color blocks? Did she decide at some point that the process, the result, or both were just too boring?

Many viewers, looking at historic quilts, misunderstand the meaning of the use of multiple fabrics in a quilt. They assume that the maker ran out of a particular fabric and had to substitute, or that she couldn't afford to buy new fabric for a quilt. But quiltmakers of the past seem to have approached the craft for the same reasons we do. They simply derive joy from sewing together pieces of fabric to create pleasing results.

We'll never know whether the maker of this quilt knew from the beginning how she would arrange her fabric or if she allowed her design decisions to evolve during the construction process. But she seems to have enjoyed her experiments, making vibrant stacks of pink-and-white and blue-and-white stripes cut on the bias, creating secondary patterns of Maltese crosses or octagons, or floating the orange center in a sea of gray. The small size of the quilt, 68½″ × 69½″, suggests that it wouldn't have been a very practical bedcover. The maker seems to have used the Pineapple pattern to explore its design possibilities, and when she had her fill of fun with it, she laid out her blocks and sewed them together.

A quilt constructed as a single Pineapple block (page 14) stands as a particular tour de force. In this case, we know for certain that the maker intended this result from the beginning. Instead of piecing her blocks onto a foundation to make the top, which would then be layered and quilted with batting and backing, this confident, unknown maker did something different. She started by placing a small square in the center of the wrong side of a large square of fabric that served simultaneously as foundation, backing, and binding. Seen from the back, the pattern of stitching resembles flat-quilted examples of foundation piecing. But here those lines of stitching indicate the seams attaching the strips, and, hidden under the folds, they are invisible from the front.

We can imagine the maker piecing lengths of printed fabric for the large square, arranging the first small pieces in the center, draping the extra over her sewing machine table, making sure that the corners of the large square don't get folded under and sewn in unintentionally. As she added strips, she used the same fabrics in each concentric layer, and

she had the skill and experience to keep the patchwork flat, avoiding ripples and tucks that would distort the design.

This maker could have simplified her task by using fewer, wider strips, but she didn't take the easy way out. We have no way of knowing how many times, if any, she may have had to stop and rip out a seam that wandered or picked up a hitchhiker; but such hindrances didn't distract her from her purpose. The identity of the maker has become separated from her work, but this quilt survives as a testament to her ingenuity, skill, and determination, whoever she was.

Pineapple quilt, collection of author, circa 1880, 77" square

INTRODUCTION

Of the many reasons people are drawn to quilting, my craving for fabric is the reason I create bed quilts. I want to be involved with fabric—to see it, touch it, and sew it. This passion is something I realize is deep within me. It is something I will never give up. The moment I sit down in my sewing chair and begin to work with fabric at my machine, it is as if a spell is cast. I feel overwhelmed with serenity. I'm astonished every time I see one fabric combined with another, in a quilt, in a book, or on the ironing board; something entirely new and magical is created.

My journey as a quilter is perhaps not unlike yours. As a means to an end, I taught myself to quilt from a book. I'd accumulated scraps of fabric, which began to take up more and more precious space in my Manhattan apartment. I soon reasoned that if I were to incorporate a bit of each into one quilt, I'd have a keepsake instead of scraps and could toss the leftovers. Ha!

For fifteen years I taught quilters at Riverbank, a New York State Park along the Hudson River. The workshops unexpectedly became a laboratory for generating ideas, out of necessity, on ways to simplify methods used to make quilts.

I regard myself as a pretty good quilter with a keen interest in process. I have learned that there is something about process that engages my mental faculties and results, by happenstance, in some surprising innovations. This book, like my two previous books, is the result of creative explorations. The greatest pleasure for me comes from seeing the work of my friends and students. I never cease to marvel at their ideas and am both excited and contented to see how they have brought life to fabric.

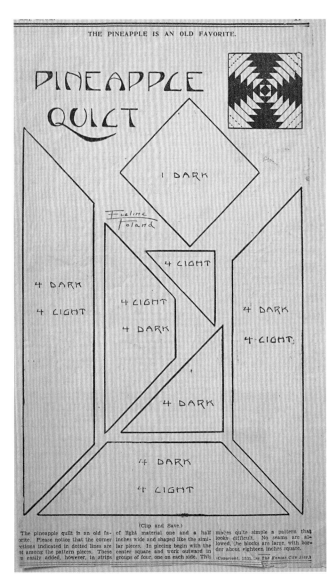

Eveline Foland's Pineapple pattern appeared in *The Kansas City Star* in 1931 (see enlargement of instructions below). She found it to be a simple pattern that looks difficult. Imagine what she could have done with a rotary cutter.

(Clip and Save.)

The pineapple quilt is an old favorite. Please notice that the corner sections indicated in dotted lines are not among the pattern pieces. These are easily added, however, in strips of light material one and a half inches wide and shaped like the similar pieces. In piecing begin with the center square and work outward in groups of four, one on each side. This makes quite simple a pattern that looks difficult. No seams are allowed, the blocks are large, with border about eighteen inches square.

(Copyright, 1931, by The Kansas City Star.)

Large Pineapple block, collection of author, foundation pieced, circa 1880, 23″ × 22½″

Large Pineapple block (back)

Large Pineapple block (back, viewed over lightbox) reveals fabric strips not scrupulously trimmed during construction.

What is your #1 piece of advice?

A: Always practice by making a sample block first, and never cut more fabric than you need to make a sample. Things happen, and like pancakes, the second one always turns out better.

Why are there paper patterns in the book?

A: Other than the Self-Mitered Log Cabin (page 88), a flip-and-sew block, all of the patterns are cutting or trimming patterns.

Isn't photocopying the cutting patterns a waste of money?

A: To make 50 blocks, cutting through 10 stacks of 5 squares of fabric requires 10 sheets of paper. Today that could cost less than a dime. Instead, consider the fabric saved because of this efficient no-waste method.

Does cutting paper dull a rotary blade?

A: Yes. Work with two medium-size rotary cutters: one for paper and one for fabric. Reuse dull fabric blades in the rotary cutter designated for paper.

On which side of an acrylic ruler should temporary guidelines be marked by permanent pen?

A: The unprinted side, so that nail polish remover or alcohol won't disturb any manufacturers' marks when the ruler is cleaned.

How many squares of fabric should be stacked at one time?

A: Start with just one or two squares. If you are new to this method and try cutting more at one time, you could end up with a stack of mistakes. After you're comfortable with the method, you can add more.

Do you ever tear fabric?

A: Yes, instead of cutting fabric, I tear it, as needed, into a manageable size and then rotary cut it.

Do you prefer to press your seams to one side or open?

A: I like them open for three reasons: It makes the quilt appear flat like wallpaper, I can match the seams more easily, and ridges won't form during machine quilting.

Do you use pins when constructing blocks?

A: Rarely. I attribute this to my sewing machine, which makes pinning generally unnecessary for me. When I do use pins, I prefer long-shafted, fine pins such as the flat flower pins or long glass-head pins. At times, short, sharp appliqué pins suit me.

Do you backstitch?

A: Not when seams will cross. To backstitch at the beginning of a seam, I drop my needle about three stitches forward, then sew backward for three stitches and then forward, continuously. At the most I'll have a single line of three stitches on top of one another.

Had I begun to sew at the very beginning of a seam, I would have sewn three stitches forward, then three stitches backward, then three stitches forward. There would be three lines of stitching instead of a tidy two. Also, by initially stitching inside, instead of at the edge, the fabric is less likely to be sucked down into the feed dogs.

How do you prepare fabric?

A: I launder and starch everything *except* striped fabric; I don't want to distort the stripes.

How do you launder your cotton fabrics?

A: Before starching and pressing the fabric, I machine wash (warm) and machine dry (hot). I join cut edges of the folded yardage, perpendicular to the selvages, with a machine zigzag or serger stitch into manageable fabric loops that won't tangle or fray in the washer or dryer. There are no loose ends to knot together. Afterward, I trim off the sewn edges and both selvages. I am not wasting fabric by trimming because the edges would have otherwise raveled while laundering.

Why do you starch?

A: I piece and quilt by machine, and I starch all of my fabric. Starched fabrics are easier to cut and sew. They will hold sharp creases, including those made by finger-pressing. When pressed during construction, blocks made of starched and pressed fabric will not shrink or become further distorted.

I am convinced that most quilters' accuracy problems stem from virgin fabric shrinking when first ironed during block construction rather than from a flawed ¼″ seam. Starched fabric is already predistorted before the first stitch is sewn. I wouldn't starch if I didn't get tremendous results for my efforts.

What kind of starch do you use?

A: I mix a solution of 50 percent water and 50 percent bottled liquid starch for yardage. I cheat at times by spray-starching small pieces of fabric without prior laundering. These pieces shrink on contact with a hot iron, which serves the purpose.

How do you starch the yardage?

A: Separate light fabrics from dark to avoid possible color transfer or bleeding. Stuff the fabric into small plastic bags, and then pour in the starch solution. The amount of solution you will need varies with the quantity and type of the fabric. Squeeze any excess air out of the bag and close it. The goal is to lightly dampen the fabric but not to soak it. Put the bag in the refrigerator. The starch solution will be distributed through all of the fabric in the bag by osmosis.

After a few hours, remove the fabric from the bag. Roll each piece individually, then return all to the bag and refrigerate again. If starch dries your skin, wear waterproof gloves.

The goal is fabric that is lightly and evenly damp, but not soaking wet. In this step, excessively damp fabric comes into contact with dry fabric.

If the fabric is too dry, add more starch solution; if the fabric is too wet, add some dry fabric. You'll soon get the hang of it. The damp fabric will keep for about a week in the refrigerator. If you don't iron it within a week, move the bags to the freezer to avoid mildew. Defrost in the refrigerator when the mood hits you. Chilled, damp fabric irons very easily.

You needn't mount a campaign to immediately starch all your cotton fabric. Begin by starching the oversize squares for these blocks with regular spray starch—*not* heavy starch or fabric sizing. Heat the fabric with the iron first, and then spray the starch. The warm fabric will absorb the starch more readily. When dried, press and repeat the process with one or two more coats of starch. You want fabric with the consistency of paper, flexible but not stiff.

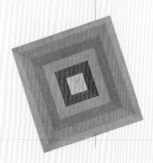

Pressing dark fabrics right side down will prevent white flakes of starch from forming on the right side. A hot, rather than a warm, soleplate is less likely to stick to damp fabric.

Starch residue develops when an iron isn't hot enough. To clean the soleplate, wipe an iron clean with a water-dampened rag. For serious buildup use a commercial cleaner such as Iron-Off by Dritz.

I use an old dry iron for three reasons:

1. There are no holes in the soleplate, so more of the surface comes into contact with fabric.

2. Both old and new irons have cotton and non-cotton settings, but I believe old irons reach a higher temperature than new ones. I find a hot iron most effective on cotton. Secondhand irons are easy to come by. Many lingered in their original boxes when they were replaced with irons that weighed less. I am not bothered by the weight of an iron. My ironing surface is low, below my waist, so my arm needn't bend very much; also, I don't iron for extended periods of time.

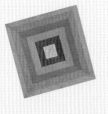

3. Sometimes brownish water will spurt from an iron. Even when water isn't added into a steam iron, moisture may seep out.

Moisture, whether from fabric dampened by water or spray, vaporizes and travels up into the iron by way of the holes in the soleplate, to be spit out later as brownish spots on the fabric. That won't happen if there are no holes in the soleplate.

Did you know that because starched and pressed fabric is flatter than fabric on the bolt, you're able to store more of it on your shelves? Hooray!

What are *rough-cut squares,* and why are they used?

A: Rough-cut squares are fabric that is cut or torn larger than needed, typically 1″ larger than its final trim size. They needn't be true squares, particularly when a scrap is used.

When rough-cut pieces are starched, stacked, and well pressed together *before* being trimmed to size, they will be reliably identical in size. Also, it is easier to prepare and accurately trim roughly cut pieces of fabric instead of cumbersome pieces of yardage. The trim size is the exact dimensions that a stack of rough-cut pieces of fabric is cut, with or without the use of a cutting pattern.

What size seam allowance is used?

A: Unless noted, a ¼″ seam allowance is used throughout this book.

NO PATIENCE BLOCK

Patience Corners, by author, 2000, 54″ square

Private collection, Buffalo, New York

In 1999 I was asked to make a quilt for a benefit auction. I wanted to use large-print Asian fabrics from my collection. I decided on the Patience Corners block because its square units had a large enough area that the large motifs would be readable. I began making the sub-units, conventionally sewing precisely cut 2″ strips to four squares 3½″ × 3½″. The sewing bored me, and while my mind wandered, I suddenly envisioned the four 3½″ squares as a 7″ square. So, I framed a 7″ square with 2″ lattice, quartered it, switched only the position of two subunits, dubbed the quilt *No Patience,* and began teaching a class called Cut-As-You-Go. Of note: Directional fabric keeps its orientation because half of the block's square subunits, though swapped, are never rotated.

Eight years later, while at work on the *Gray No Patience* quilt (page 25), I found another way to increase block speed with a construction technique that wasted no fabric: the Square Cut method. Quick and efficient, its four 2″ rotary cuts yield two blocks for every pair of 11″ squares of fabric.

The conventional method uses a square and two cut-to-size rectangles.

The Cut-As-You-Go method (pages 21–22) accommodates fabrics of limited sizes (2″-wide strips and 7″ squares) and is ideal when the lattice or the squares (but not both) use a fabric repeatedly.

The Square Cut method (pages 23–24) is fast and frugal.

Making Basic No Patience Blocks

CUT-AS-YOU-GO METHOD

Rough-cut fabric square: 7½" minimum

Fabric square trim size: 7"

Unfinished block size: 9½" square

Finished block size: 9" square

1 Rough-cut one piece of starched and pressed fabric to 7½" square. Trim to make a 7" square.

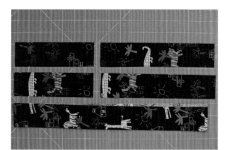

2 Framing strips. The square is framed by 2"-wide strips. Mathematically, 2 strips 2" × 7" and 2 strips 2" × 10" are cut from a 2" × 34" fabric length. *Instead,* using scissors, cut a 2" × 36"–minimum-length strip into the framing strips as you sew. An even more generous length permits isolating, positioning, and sewing a specific motif from the framing strip to the square. Join smaller leftover strips into usable pieces.

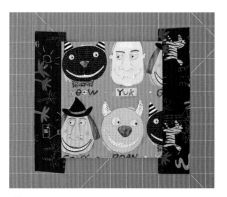

3 Sew framing strips to any 2 opposite sides of the square.

4 Press seams. Trim strips flush with the square.

5 Sew strips to the other sides. Press.

6 Trim block to 10" square.

7 Center the block on the mat gridlines. They serve as vertical and horizontal cutting guidelines. Cut the block into equal quarters, 5″ square. If a block is an oversized 10″ square or slightly irregular, using the gridlines is a simple way to cut the blocks into quarters fair and mostly square.

8 Switch the units at the lower left and upper right. Don't turn them upside down, and don't turn them around; just switch them.

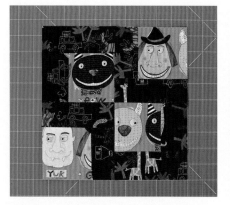

The blue monster is in the lower left position; the framing strips form a left-leaning figure eight.

9 Alternatively, switch the lower right and upper left units.

The blue monster and the witch haven't moved, but the animals have switched positions. A right-leaning figure eight is formed.

Warning: A sewn block using *nondirectional* fabric for the center square can be rotated into a left- or right-leaning figure eight. But if you are using *directional* fabric, decide whether the block will be left- or right-leaning before sewing the 4 units together; the directional fabric will appear sideways if it's rotated after being sewn.

10 Arrange the 4 block units at the sewing machine. Sew 2 units together, press, and return them to the layout. Repeat with the remaining pair. Sew the halves together after checking that a figure eight is formed. Press.

Switch to correct placement.

Warning: Incorrect placement of halves—a mistake in the making!

SQUARE CUT METHOD

Rough-cut fabric square: 12″ minimum

Fabric square trim size: 11″

Unfinished block size: 9½″ square

Finished block size: 9″ square

1 Rough-cut 2 different 12″ squares. Starch and press the 2 squares. Layer them right sides up on a mat; trim the stack to 11″ square.

2 Make successive 2″ cuts vertically through the stack (cutting the 2 longest strips first), using one of the layouts shown below.

For a pair of fabric squares, 4 cuts of 2″ yield 8 rectangles plus two 7″ squares.

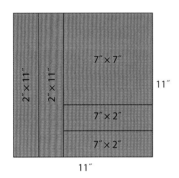

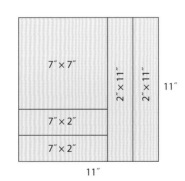

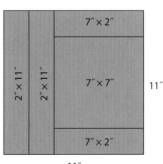

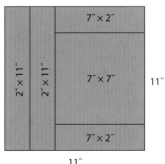

Note

Remember, the *rough-cut* squares (page 19) are cut larger than needed. The squares are then starched and pressed together before being trimmed to their final accurate size.

Pictured are 5 cutting options. Choose an arrangement that is comfortable for you to rotary cut or that results in a 7″ square from a specific area of the fabric. Right-handers tend to cut vertically from the left side, and left-handers from the right.

3 Sew the 7″ × 2″ rectangles to any opposite sides of the 7″ squares and press; sew on the remaining rectangles. Press.

4 Trim the block to 10″ square.

5 Cut the block, centered on the mat's gridlines, into equal quarters, 5″ square.

6 Recombine the block, and sew the units together (Steps 8–10, page 22).

📎 Note

Two 11″ squares of fabric yield the pieces for 2 blocks; 50 squares yield 50 blocks. Sets of strips and squares may be combined into other sets of blocks (robbing Peter to pay Paul) or into random assortments. Each ⅓ yard (12″ × 40″) of fabric yields 3 rough-cut 12″ squares.

Alternate option

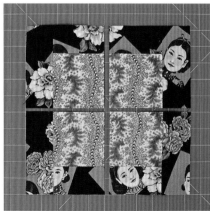

No Patience Design Ideas

ROOM TO BREATHE

I created some open space for the *Strippy No Patience* quilt (below) by adding vertical sashing strips (finishing 4½″ wide) between the vertical rows of 9″ finished blocks. The sashing gave the quilt upward direction and movement, while cutting down on the number of blocks to be pieced.

I added visual relief (breathing space) to the *Gray No Patience* quilt with three alternate blocks. The frames are cut 2″ wide, and the center piece is cut 6½″ square. Cut a 6½″ square from a leftover 7″ square or from a different fabric. I pieced one 6½″ square from two small scraps.

Gray No Patience, made by author; quilted by Janice E. Petre, Sinking Spring, Pennsylvania; 2008, 73½″ × 82½″

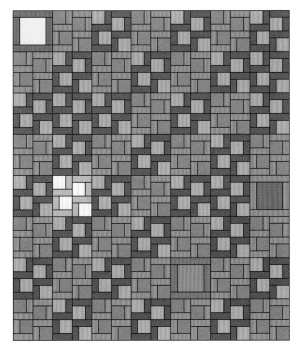

Alternate block from *Gray No Patience* quilt

Strippy No Patience, by author, 2000, 61″ × 74″

Layout for *Gray No Patience*

ISOLATING A MOTIF *(Optional)*

This is one way to control images that will appear in the four windows of a block: Create preview windows on a 12½″ square ruler.

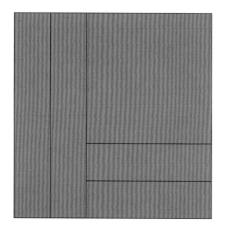

1 Plan to isolate the 7″ square from the upper right position of the fabric.

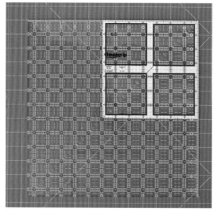

2 Temporarily tape or glue the 7″ Window Template (page 98) to the bottom of the ruler. Use a permanent marker to trace the outline of the dark windows onto the top of a 12½″ square ruler.

3 Move the marked ruler over an expanse of fabric, and pinpoint the desired motifs.

The 11″ cut square with desired motif in upper right corner

Motifs within the in-progress block

Making Super-Sized No Patience Blocks

Quick-cut an interesting 15″ finished block with a variation of the Square Cut method (pages 23–24).

Rough-cut fabric square: 18″ minimum

Fabric square trim size: 17″

Unfinished block size: 15½″ square

Finished block size: 15″ square

 Tip

In lieu of a large ruler and a large rotary mat, consider folding the fabric into fourths and using an available ruler to trim the folded fabric into a square that's half the desired size. The fabric, when unfolded, will be the desired size (see page 28).

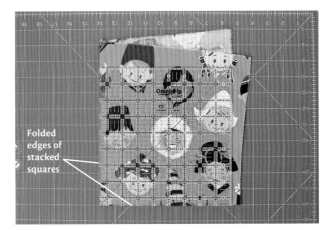

1 Rough-cut 2 squares, each 18″, from starched and pressed fabric. Fold them individually into fourths (fold in half, then again crosswise in half), and stack them with their folded sides aligned. True up the stack to 8½″ square by trimming off both raw (*not folded*) edges.

As folded, the stack is 8½″ square; unfolded it is 17″ square.

2 Cut 1 strip 3″ wide along a *raw* edge. Then cut a second strip 3″ wide along the short *raw* edge.

Note

The result of two rotary cuts through two folded squares is ten pieces. If cutting through the eight layers of fabric is intimidating, cut through only one folded square, which is four layers, at a time.

Two folded 5½″ squares will emerge from the folded sides. They open to 11″ square. The small rectangles are 3″ × 5½″ folded and open to 3″ × 11″. The large rectangles are 3″ × 8½″ folded and open to 3″ × 17″.

3 Lay out the pieces.

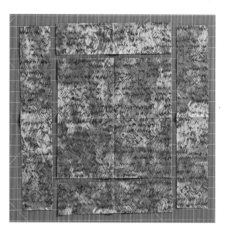

4 Switch the squares between the 2 fabric groups. Lay out the first block.

5 Sew the short rectangles to any opposite sides of the square and press; sew on the remaining rectangles. Press. Trim the block, centered on the mat's gridlines, to 16″ square.

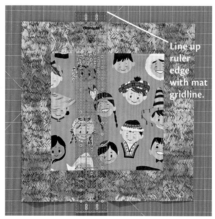

Line up ruler edge with mat gridline.

6 Cut the block into equal quarters, each 8″ square, guided by the mat's gridlines.

7 Recombine the pieces and sew into a left- or right-leaning figure eight (Steps 8–10, page 22). Repeat for the remaining units, or incorporate them among other fabrics.

8 Repeat Steps 3–7 to sew, cut, and recombine units, and sew the other block combination.

Large-scale prints are proportionally suited for super-sized blocks. The block pictured is 15″ square, finished.

An arrangement of four No Patience blocks

Patience Corners (page 20). Back was pieced from two fabrics.

Ghanian Lyric, made by Betty A. Davis; quilted by Flora Richmond, New York, New York; 2009, 64½″ × 57″

Made of hand-dyed cotton batiks from Ghana, West Africa

Make It Simpler No Patience Measurement Guide

BLOCK TYPE	START	CUTS	JOIN STRIPS	RECOMBINE, SEW
Conventional: 9″ square		4 squares 3½″, 4 rectangles 2″ × 3½″, 4 rectangles 2″ × 5″		Unfinished block: 9½″ square
Cut-As-You-Go: 9″ square	Rough-cut one 7½″ square. Trim to 7″ square.	Cut variable-length strip 2″ wide.	Size of block with strips sewn: 10″ square	Unfinished block: 9½″ square
Square Cut: 9″ square	Rough-cut two 12″ squares. Trim to 11″ square.	Cuts 2″ wide	Size of block with strips sewn: 10″ square	Unfinished block: 9½″ square
Super-Sized: 15″ square	Rough-cut two 18″ squares, fold into quarters. Trim raw edges to 8½″ square.	Cuts 3″ wide	Size of block with strips sewn: 16″ square	Unfinished block: 15½″ square
Alternate: 9″ square	Cut one 6½″ square.	Cut strips 2″ wide.		Unfinished block: 9½″ square

No Patience blocks

The Red Xcentric Concentric Sampler, made by author; quilted by Janice E. Petre, Sinking Spring, Pennsylvania; 2004–2008, 60″ × 80″

Barbara Johannah devised a method of piecing quarter-square triangle blocks, which just about every machine piecer has embraced. A variation of the technique was introduced independently by Mary Ellen Hopkins.

Here is the overview of piecing quarter-square triangle blocks from squares rather than triangles.

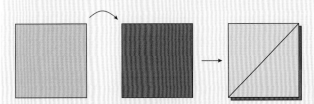

Step A: Stack 2 fabric squares, and draw a diagonal line on the top square.

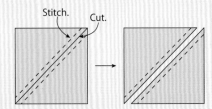

Step B: Stitch ¼″ away from the drawn line on both sides. Cut.

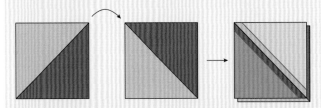

Step C: Matching seams, stack 2 half-squares.

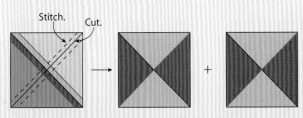

Step D: Draw a diagonal line crossing the seams. Stitch ¼″ away from the drawn line on both sides. Cut on drawn line.

Late one spring evening in 2003, I looked at tiny triangles of striped fabric on the cutting board and minutes later was dumbstruck with the Xcentric block. Close to midnight I telephoned my friend Michele, a night owl in Florida, and asked her to replicate what I'd done. Thirty minutes later she emailed images of Concentric and Xcentric units of breathtaking fabric combinations to me. She enthusiastically confirmed the units could be made without cutting or matching any triangles.

I used two *identical* 8½" squares of *striped* fabric and simultaneously ended up with a Concentric and an Xcentric unit. *No triangles were cut to make these blocks.*

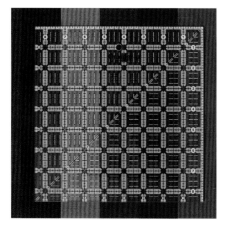 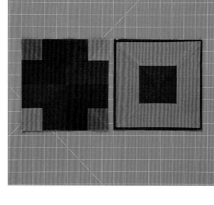

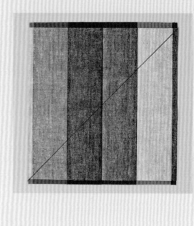

🔖 Tip

Align a pair of 8½" squares right sides together, being careful to match the stripes. This is the key step to success. In this photo, one square was intentionally cut longer to illustrate the alignment.

Then I cut four identical 8½" squares of striped fabric to make an Xcentric block consisting of two Concentric units and two Xcentric units. My extreme test was a *super-sized* two-sided quilt from 9⅓ yards of one striped fabric (page 37). Large or small, a pair of blocks takes only four seams.

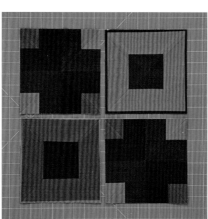

🔖 Note

Why cut 8½" squares?

Since fat quarters, long quarters, and half-yards of fabric have a width in increments of 9", then an 8½" square ruler can be used as a template, and they can be cut efficiently, with little waste.

Fabric square trim size: 8½″

Unfinished size: 7½″ square (1 unit);
14½″ square (4-unit block)

Finished size: 7″ square (1 unit);
14″ square (4-unit block)

Select ¼ yard of striped fabric with bold, contrasting, medium, *even* stripes for a pair of practice units. Good news: Don't launder, press, or starch the fabric, which might distort the stripes and throw off the automatic miters. A slight fudge factor is built into the original 8½″ square cuts to compensate for shrinkage from pressing during construction. The many varieties of striped fabric result in surprising, curious, and at first unpredictable compositions.

> ✿ **Note**
>
> You won't get as many identical squares from fabric with wide stripes as you will from fabric with thin stripes. On the other hand, wide stripes are easier to align than thin stripes.

> ✿ **Tip**
>
> When shopping for fabric, use a sheet of 8½″ × 11″ paper to gauge how many 8½″ squares you can cut from a quarter yard.

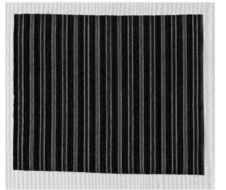

18″ × 20″ (approximate) *fat* quarter yard of woven, uneven, symmetrical striped fabric

4 identical 8½″ squares on fat quarter

9″ × 40″ (approximate) quarter yard of woven, uneven, symmetrical striped fabric

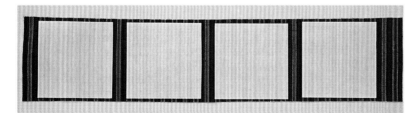

4 identical 8½″ squares on ¼ yard

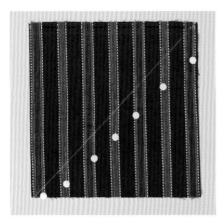

1 For the 2 practice units, cut 2 identical 8½″ squares. Draw a diagonal line on the wrong side of a fabric square. (The line won't be visible in the finished block.) Position the squares right sides together, aligning their stripes. Pin parallel to the stripes through the drawn line.

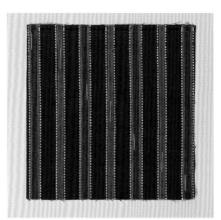

2 Check the back; the pins should register in the same area of the stripe on both the front and back.

3 Check to be sure the stripes align on both fabric squares.

4 Position a straight edge, such as a ruler, piece of cardboard, or the very thin Dritz Ezy-Hem tool, along the diagonal line. Peel back the top square. Like what you see?

5 Sew a seam ¼″ on *each* side of the diagonal line. For a foolproof and perfectly aligned center miter, instead of sewing continuously from end to end, I start in the center and sew to one corner. Then I sew from the center to the opposite corner. The remaining seam can be sewn uninterrupted, from end to end. Be careful not to sew over the angled pins. Remove the remaining pins.

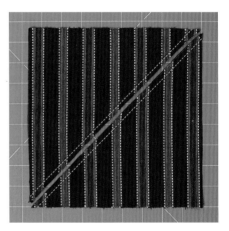

6 Cut on the marked line, between the seamlines, through both layers.

7 Arrange the triangles in identical positions. Note the long stripe at the base of the triangles and the short stripe at the top.

8 Press the seams open or to the side (I almost always press my seams open). Shown above is the back view with the seams pressed to the same side.

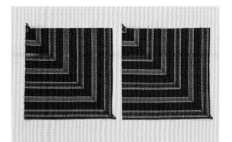

Front view

9 Mirror the blocks.

10 Flip 1 square onto the other, right sides together. Align long stripes over long stripes, short stripes over short stripes. The diagonal seams, whether pressed open or to the side, should also align.

11 Draw a diagonal line that crosses the previous seam, and pin parallel to the stripes to keep them aligned.

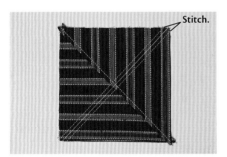

12 Sew a seam ¼″ from each side of the diagonal line. Be careful not to sew over the angled pins. Remove the remaining pins.

13 Cut on the line, between the seamlines, through both layers.

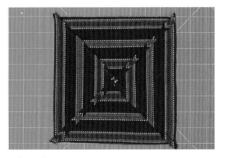

14 Press the seams open on both units.

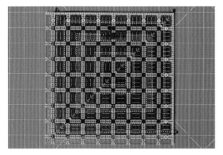

15 True up each unit to 7½″ square, centering as well as possible.

Xcentric unit (left) and Concentric unit (right)

A Study in Stripes

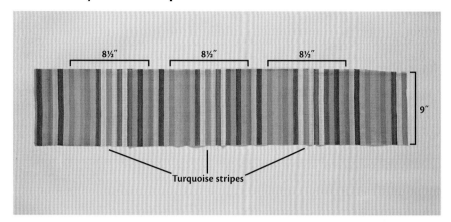

Turquoise stripes

This woven fabric is a regular, even stripe of an asymmetrically colored pattern. Four identical squares, each with turquoise stripes running through their centers, were cut from ½ yard. The turquoise stripes will appear in the center of each triangle in the following Xcentric units comprising the larger Xcentric block.

Front view of 4 units sewn together. Notice the turquoise stripes predictably run to the centers of the Xcentric units.

Computer-generated quilt from 4 units

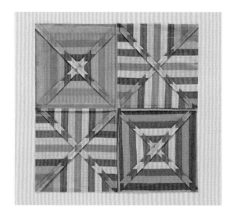

Back view of 4 units sewn together

ANATOMY OF A SUPER-SIZED QUILT

For five years I entertained the idea of making an enormous reversible quilt. I even bought red fabric paint to custom make awning stripe fabric—bought, but not opened.

In 2008, Strip-It, a collection of 2½″-wide printed stripes in an asymmetrical pattern, debuted from Marcus Fabrics. I sewed together 2 widths of it, creating a unit approximately 84″ × 168″, which I then subcut into 2 equal units of 84″ × 84″. My friends helped assemble the enormous units into Xcentric and Concentric tops; it was a great deal of fabric to handle. It took us an afternoon, the floor, 9⅓ yards of fabric, and 5 seams. Each top is over 100 times larger than the previous 7½″ square units, so it's understandable that the stripes skewed at the quilt's edges.

A printed, even stripe of an asymmetrically colored pattern. To double its width and make it symmetrical, cut 2 identical pieces. Follow the piecing instructions on pages 34–35.

Two-Sided Black and White Xcentric, by author, 2009, 73″ square

ASYMMETRIC AND IRREGULAR ECCENTRICITIES

Printed border stripe

Xcentric Concentric Avocado, by author, 2009, 40″ square

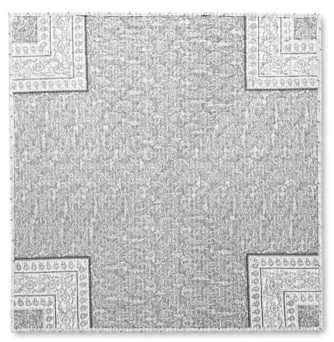

Xcentric Concentric Avocado (back)

Uneven and asymmetric printed stripe

Counting Fish (front and back), by author, 2004–2008, 40″ × 40″

USING XCENTRIC BLOCKS AS BACKGROUNDS

The blocks add interest as backgrounds or quilt cornerstones.

Sedgewick Squirrel, by Judith H. Corwin, New York, New York, 2009, 20″ square

Sedgewick is appliquéd to a Concentric square. Judy sculpted him of hand-dyed boiled wool and stuffed and hand embroidered him with golden thread; the acorn is cotton fabric and surrounded by vintage buttons.

Georgina, by Judith H. Corwin, New York, New York, 2009, 29″ × 28½″

A cloth doll rests on a quilted blanket of a Concentric square of Provençal fabric. She has a hand-embroidered face, yarn hair with a vintage button brooch, and a real pearl necklace. Georgina's skirt has a scalloped edge for detail, with antique lace slightly revealed on the edge of her slip.

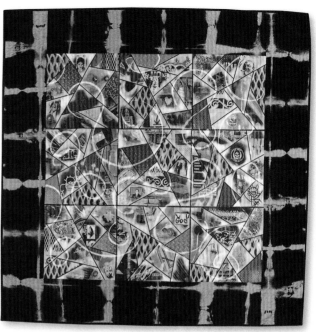

New York Graffiti V (quilt in progress), by Carol Goossens'

Carol transferred her photographs to fabric and manipulated the images with Photoshop software.

Needleturn Appliqués, by Dorothea Hahn, Port Washington, New York, 2005, each 11″ square

A pair of needleturn appliquéd tops based on Japanese crests on Xcentric and Concentric backgrounds

New York Graffiti V, by Carol Goossens', New York, New York, 2004, 32″ square

Carol completed her composition with overlaid raw-edge Xcentric appliqués.

Persian Tablecloth (detail)

Modified Xcentric blocks were set on point and framed by yo-yo units of the same fabric. Carol used only one fabric to construct this piece.

Photo by Roger LeMoine

Persian Tablecloth, by Carol Goossens', New York, New York, 2006, 46½" square

Photographed on a blue surface by Roger LeMoine

Original fabric

A couple of years later, Susan Kaletsky of New York, New York, happened to use the same fabric as Carol. Susan cut 8 identical squares to make 2 different sets of Xcentric blocks.

❧ Tip

It's efficient to cut two identical squares at a time from ½ yard of fabric. Center a long 8½″-wide ruler on a particular stripe after marking the centering line on the ruler. Cut on both long edges of the ruler. Cross cut 2 squares. Even a fabric of jumbled stripes will work with spectacular results.

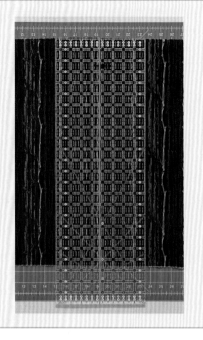

❧ Note

The blocks comprising the *Red Xcentric Concentric Sampler* quilt (page 31) were set on point. The quilt's Xcentric Four-Patch blocks measure 14½″ square unfinished, 14″ square finished. Measured on point they are under 20″ finished on their diagonals. Mathematically the 4 corner blocks are cut diagonally, once, from 2 squares, 10¾″ each, and the side blocks are cut by quartering 21″ squares diagonally. I cut setting squares larger than this math dictates. After quilting I true up the quilt, trimming away any excess.

G's Squared, made by Michele Shatz, Boynton Beach, Florida; additional quilting by Barbara Lacey, Davie, Florida; 2005, 57″ square

Classroom in The City Quilter, New York, New York

Sew Before You Cut!

Liberty Arrowhead, made by author; quilted by Janice E. Petre, Sinking Spring, Pennsylvania; 2008, 77″ square

The Arrowhead is a traditionally pieced block that appeared in *The Kansas City Star* newspaper on March 26, 1941. My 9″ unfinished Arrowhead block is made entirely from two fabric squares, 8″ each, cut from starched yardage. Sew two squares of fabric together and make three cuts; ten perfectly presewn subunits will appear before your eyes. There is no wasted fabric, and, without planning, four pointed asymmetrical units are magically prefabricated. The center of each block is a four-patch. The blocks in alternating vertical rows of the quilt top may be rotated or set identically.

Making the Block

Rough-cut fabric square: 8½″ minimum

Fabric square trim size: 8″

Unfinished block size: 9″ square

Finished block size: 8½″ square

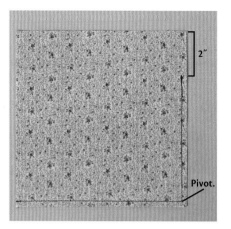

2″

Pivot.

1 A pair of rough-cut squares, 8½″ minimum (along the straight of grain), stacked and starched with right sides together, trimmed to 8″square. They should be sewn (Step 2) before they shift out of alignment.

🕷 Note

If the rough-cut squares are of previously starched yardage, they must be restarched.

Starching or restarching pairs of rough-cut fabric squares and ironing them together keeps them aligned for cutting into exact 8″ square units before sewing an accurate ¼″ seam around the outside edge. Starch with caution because some fabrics might bleed.

2 With a shorter stitch length (see Glossary, pages 96–97) and starting with a backstitch, begin sewing a ¼″ seam allowance 2″ from the top right edge. Pivot ¼″ from the bottom, and continue sewing to the very edge of the fabric square. Backstitch.

🕷 Tip

1. To determine where to start stitching, rather than tediously measuring off the 2″ gap, use a 2″ sticky note; 1⅞″ sticky notes are acceptable.

2. Sew along the right and bottom edges; pivot, if possible, to avoid unpicking a stitch or two later on if pressing the seam open.

3. Reposition the sticky note to the lower left edge to complete the edge sewing.

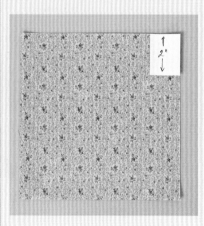

↑
2″
↓

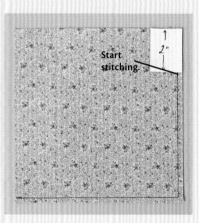

↑
2″
↓

Start stitching.

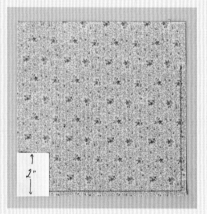

↑
2″
↓

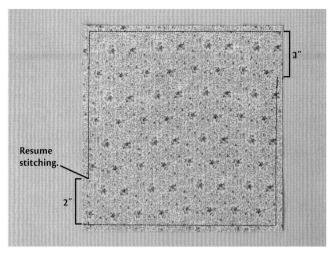

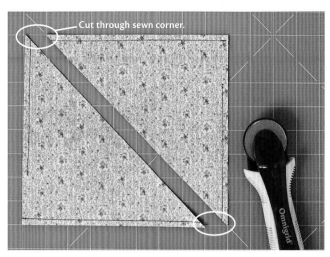

Cut through sewn corner.

3 Resume sewing, in the same manner, 2" from the bottom edge and finish at the top right corner.

4 Cut the sewn unit diagonally through both completely sewn corners.

🎀 Note

If you cut the wrong diagonal, see Mistakes Happen (page 47) for a solution.

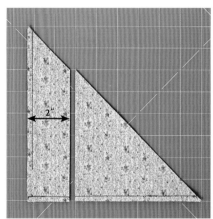

5 Stack both triangle units, aligning the seamlines. It doesn't matter which triangle is on the bottom or on the top or how they face, as long as the seams line up.

6 Cut a 2"-wide strip, parallel to one stitched edge, through the 4 layers of fabric. Do not disturb the stack.

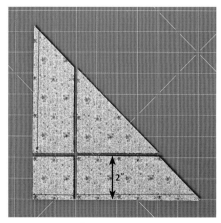

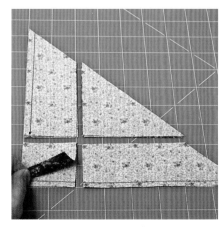

7 Cut a 2"-wide strip, parallel to the other stitched edge.

A peek within the stack

Bingo! Presewn patches revealed.

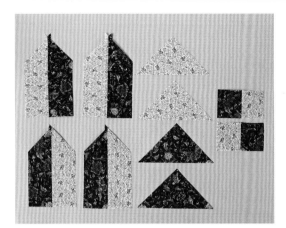

8 Ten perfect subunits. Press the seams; don't use starch or steam. I press the seams *open*.

9 Arrange the 10 subunits—identical fabrics never adjoin each other. The pairs of squares and arrow pieces should measure 3½″ wide.

Note

The block's interior units are sewn on the straight of grain of the fabric squares. The bias outside edges of the block are stable because the fabric squares were initially starched. If necessary, fuse strips of nonwoven interfacing to the edges of the quilt top's perimeter to stabilize it.

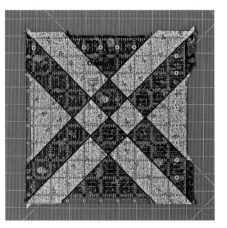

10 Sew the center four-patch first. It will measure 3½″ square. Sew the middle diagonal row. Sew the remaining diagonal rows. Press as you go.

11 Sew the remaining 2 seams. Press with the straight of grain of the fabric.

12 True up the block, aligning diagonals as best as possible with a homemade ruler guide (see Note below).

Note

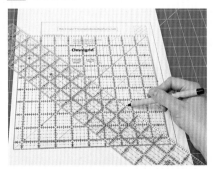

9″ Unfinished Arrowhead Block True-Up Guide

Create a true-up ruler by tracing the 9″ Unfinished Arrowhead Block True-Up Guide (page 100). Mark off a 9″ square area on a ruler. Draw diagonal lines from corner to corner to mark an X. Draw lines 1½″ away on each side of each diagonal line to add four lines. A 9″ square guide won't entirely fit in an 8½″ book, so extend the pattern lines.

Trimmed block measures 9″ square.

SURPRISE, SURPRISE

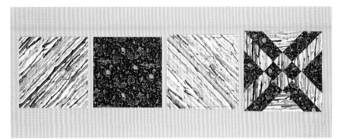

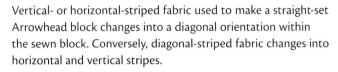

Vertical- or horizontal-striped fabric used to make a straight-set Arrowhead block changes into a diagonal orientation within the sewn block. Conversely, diagonal-striped fabric changes into horizontal and vertical stripes.

MISTAKES HAPPEN

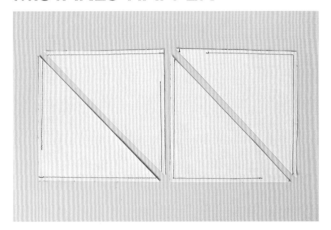

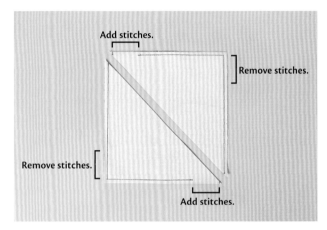

The unit on the left was cut correctly, through the *completely sewn* corners. The unit on the right was—oops!—cut by *mistake* through the partially sewn corners.

Save fabric. To salvage a miscut block, remove 2″ of stitches from 2 sewn areas and sew 2 other areas, as shown. Be sure to match the placement of the reworked pieces to the photos (page 45) to cut the remaining units.

Arrowhead Piece Talks, made by Laura Yellen Catlan, Huntington, New York; quilted by Janice E. Petre, Sinking Spring, Pennsylvania; 2009, 85½″ square

Bali Straight Arrow, by Lois Podolny, Tucson, Arizona, 2009, 56½" × 67"

Note the additional arrowhead blocks in both side borders.

OLD ITALIAN BLOCK

Old Italian Block, by author, 2004, 70″ × 76″

Make two pairs of parallel rotary cuts through a stack of trimmed fabric squares using *only* a mat to measure—no waste. That's it! Two 8″ squares of fabric yield the *18 pieces* for two 6″ finished blocks, lightning fast.

It's a snap to figure yardage for an Old Italian Block quilt. Every 6″ finished block begins as a trimmed 8″ fabric square. A quilt of 100 blocks uses 100 trimmed squares. A quarter-yard's worth of fabric yields 4 blocks.

Making the Blocks

Rough-cut fabric square: 8½″ minimum

Fabric square trim size: 8″

Unfinished block size: 6½″ square

Finished block size: 6″ square

CUTTING

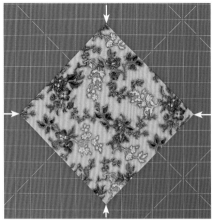

1 Rough-cut 2 different fabric squares (page 97) to 8½″. It doesn't matter if the right sides are together or not. Starch and press together. Trim the stack of fabric squares to 8″.

2 Position the squares on point on the cutting mat gridlines.

> ☠ **Note**
>
> If you align any three corners on gridlines, the fourth will line up by itself!

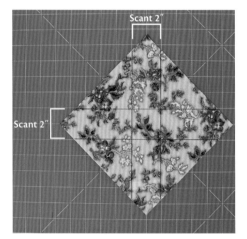

Scant 2″

Scant 2″

3 Cut perpendicular scant 2″-wide channels, through the center of the squares, along the mat's gridlines, following Steps A–D (to the right).

> ☠ **Note**
>
> The mat gridlines are 1″ apart. Instead of cutting directly on a gridline, cut just inside of the line, toward the tip of the fabric squares. By shaving off a hair from each line, the channel will be a scant 2″ wide. Mark the intended mat gridlines with chalk to avoid accidentally cutting along the wrong gridline.

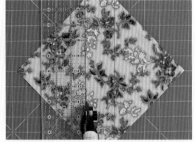

A. Make the first cut.

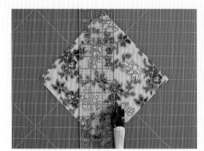

B. Make a second cut.

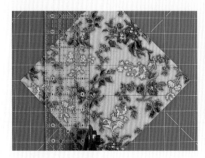

C. Rotate the mat and make a third cut.

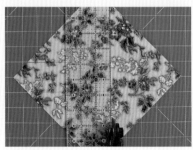

D. Rotate the mat and make the fourth cut. All of the pieces, except for the triangles, are a scant 2″ wide—18 pieces from 2 fabric squares. Awesome.

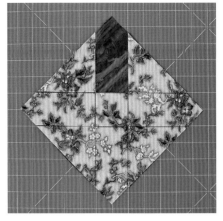

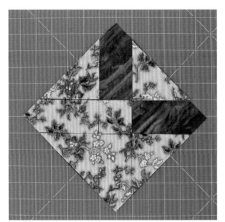

Unveiling one of two blocks

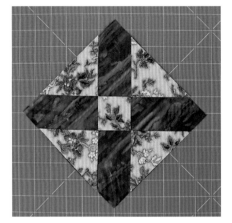

Store a stack of pieces in an 8″ or larger square container.

🐾 Note

Squares that were cut together need not be partnered together. When many different fabrics are cut, the assorted pieces can be assembled into different combinations.

4 Lay out the pieces for one block.

5 Sew into 3 sections, pressing as you go.

6 Sew the sections together. Press.

7 Lay out the pieces for the second block.

8 Repeat sewing and pressing for the second block.

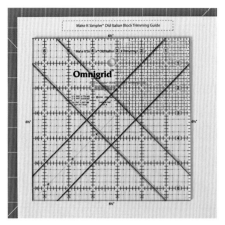

9 Mark guidelines on a 6½″ square ruler using the pattern (page 99).

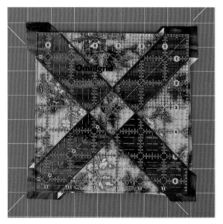

10 True up the block to 6½″ square.

Completed, trimmed blocks

Note

An interesting design element occurs when fabric squares are cut in this manner. Notice the batik's directional pattern in the blocks; its stripes run continuously across the block.

Note

To paper piece this block, photocopy and prepare the foundation pattern on page 109 in my first book *Make It Simpler Paper Piecing* (C&T Publishing). It's incredibly fast to paper piece this block because it's nearly a no-sew block. Just glue all 9 pieces to the foundation, fold, and sew the 4 long X seams. Assemble several blocks for sewing at once. Because all 9 sub-units are *unpieced*, there is a further shortcut. Spray a repositionable fabric-to-paper adhesive, such as 404 Spray and Fix, onto several folded foundations. Stick the pieces in place on the foundations, and sew the 4 seams. Note: The foundation pattern is too wide to fit entirely on an 8½″ sheet of vellum—its dashed lines won't fit, but they are unnecessary.

Old Italian Block quilt, collection of author,
circa 1875–1899, 39½″ square

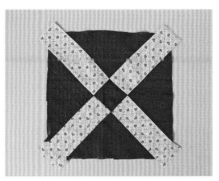

Red and yellow Old Italian Block, collection
of author, circa late nineteenth to early
twentieth century

Red and yellow Old Italian Block (back)

Construction notes: The fabric was torn
and a strip of yellow was combined from
2 pieces. The outside edges of the block
are all on bias. Left unfinished, trueing-up
this block would have required carving
the rectangles into arrow-shaped pieces.

Tip

Conserve fabric. Sew undersize pieces into oversize
squares for *any* Make It Simpler rough-cut block.
Press seams open and flatten with spray starch
before trimming to size.

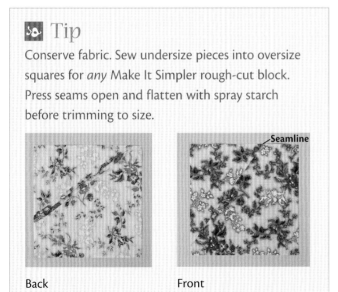

Back   Front

Seamline

Old Italian Block,
collection of
author, circa late
nineteenth century

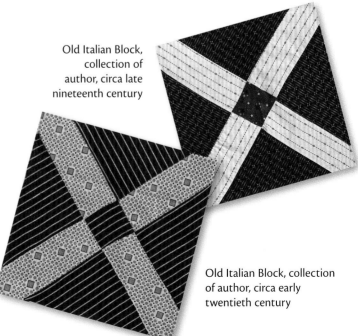

Old Italian Block, collection
of author, circa early
twentieth century

My Father's Legacy, by Renée Kane Fields,
Astoria, New York, 2009, 60½" × 48½"

Renée used a different method for cutting
the blocks. The batik X shapes were cut as
crosswise strips from yardage. The Asian background fabrics were quick-cut as described in
this chapter. Renée saved the leftover Asian
fabric X pieces for a future project.

Gael devised a clever construction method
independent of the technique I use. She
stacked 2 squares of fabric, cut diagonally
through the center, switched the strips,
and sewed the blocks together. After
pressing and restacking, she repeated the
process, cutting the diagonal strip from
the opposite direction. She pieced the pairs
back together and trimmed them to size.
It's a slick operation that creates fixed pairs
of opposing fabrics.

Road to Cork, by Gael O'Donnell,
Te Marua, New Zealand, 2008, 86" square

Photo courtesy of *New Zealand Quilter*, Wellington, New Zealand
Photo by John Bellamy

Gray Windmill, by author, 2008, 36½″ × 42½″

A block in the quilt is merely 4 pieces of *different* fabrics sewn together into a *square*.

F rom a design aspect, a Windmill block spins across the surface of the quilt. From a sewing standpoint, the block is a total dream come true. Unlike an ordinary Four-Patch block, it doesn't matter whether or not the corners of these blocks meet when the top is sewn together. Because the sewn block is trimmed to size, it's 99 percent foolproof. The extraordinarily simple cutting gives you more time to be creative with fabric.

Yardage calculations are simple. One rough-cut 8″ square yields a 6″ square finished block. Make these using multiples of any four fabrics to create the four-bladed windmill effect.

No-Waste Windmill block detail

Each windmill piece has only one right angle; it's a corner of the fabric square from which it was cut.

Making the Block

Rough-cut fabric square: 8″ minimum

Fabric square trim size: 7½″

Unfinished block size: 6½″ square

Finished block size: 6″ square

CUTTING

For more cutting options, see pages 60–62.

To create the pieces for this block, cut on the lines of a paper pattern laid on top of rough-cut fabric squares.

🪡 Note

If a fabric square is placed right-side down (big mistake) when cut, the pieces will spin the wrong way, unless the fabric is reversible.

The big mistake, fabric was cut right side down.

Note

Since fabric squares and the pattern *must* be right sides up, apply the fabric or repositionable gluestick sparingly to the pattern to avoid residue on the fabric.

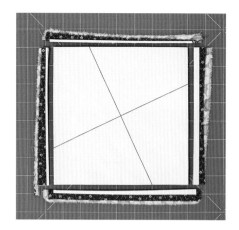

1 Photocopy the Windmill Cutting Pattern (page 101). Roughly trim its margin down to ¼". Rough-cut (page 97) a stack of starched 8" fabric squares, *right sides up*. Lightly glue the cutting pattern to the stack.

2 Trim around the outside edge of the stack, through the lines of the pattern.

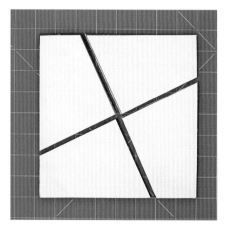

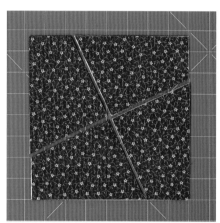

3 Keep the stack intact while cutting through the 2 interior *black* pattern guidelines. The supplemental *dashed* lines will facilitate centering the cutting pattern should you ever wish to resize the blocks.

Bingo! Block pieces revealed.

4 Throw away the papers.

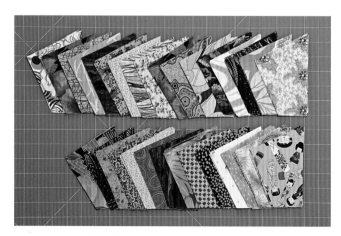

Assortment of cut pieces

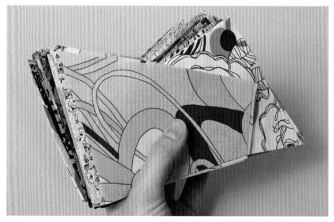

Assortment in hand

ARRANGING THE PIECES

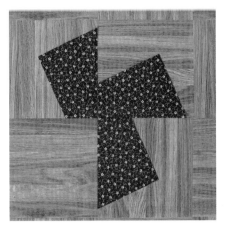

1 Position a piece as shown, right side up. A gridded surface works well to help line up the pieces. In this case, it's a floor.

2 Position a second piece of the same fabric.

3 Position the third piece.

4 Position the fourth piece.

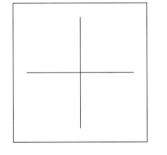

◦ Note

To arrange the pieces on an ungridded surface—such as a design wall, a bed, or a tabletop—draw an imaginary cross to align the initial nest of pieces.

5 Position the next 4 pieces.

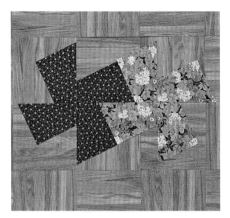

6 Position the next 4 pieces.

7 Add 4 more pieces, for 16 pieces total, enough to see an emerging quilt. Notice the exposed angular areas around the outside edges of the block? That's where border pieces will fit to frame the quilt top.

Arrangement on design wall

🕯 Tip

Lay out all of the pieces first, and then rearrange them.

🕯 Tip

Over time, arrange *all* the pieces. Resist the impulse to sew any blocks before the top is finally arranged, including the border pieces. To do so would make it difficult to rearrange sewn pieces and may throw off the grid's symmetry. You have been warned!

SEWING THE BLOCK

The block that is sewn is actually square in shape.

1 Choose the pieces for the first block.

Stitch.

2 Flip a piece over onto an adjoining piece, right sides together. Align the 2 pieces, matching the edges at the center intersection of the block. Stitch from this center point to the outer edge. Pinning is unnecessary; the edge of the block, where the seam ends, will eventually be trimmed off.

3 Return the pieces to the arrangement to keep the block in order. Sew the remaining pieces together for the other half of the block. Press the seam allowances of both halves open.

Align intersections.

4 Align the halves. Match the intersection of the previously sewn seams (center). The outside edges of the block won't line up exactly; you'll trim it later.

Tip

Match the center intersection and hold it together with your fingertips instead of a pin. Position this center intersection about ⅛" ahead of the needle, and immediately lower the needle into it. The needle holds the intersection in place. Sew the seam from this center point to the edge of the block. Remove the block from the machine and cut the threads. Then, start from the center and stitch to the other end to complete the seam. The center will be as close to perfection as possible; if not, it will still be pleasing to the eye.

5 Stitch the center seam, and press open. The corners are intended to be oversized; they will be trimmed later.

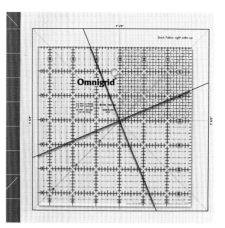

6 Mark guidelines on a 6½″ square ruler using the cutting pattern (page 101) and a permanent marker (the marker can easily be removed with alcohol).

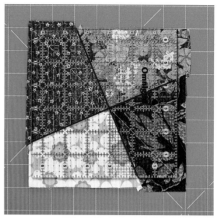

7 Align the guidelines over the diagonal seamlines and true up the block to 6½″ square.

Completed block

Alternate Cutting Options

If you don't want to photocopy multiple cutting patterns, here are two other cutting options. After the windmill pieces are cut, follow the instructions on pages 57–60 to arrange and sew the blocks.

OPTION 1: PAPERLESS GUIDED CUTTING

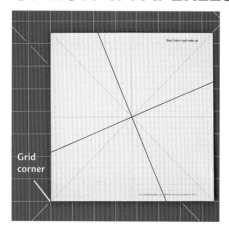

Grid corner

1 Align a copy of the Windmill Cutting Pattern (page 101) on the cutting mat at a corner intersection. A slight dab of nonpermanent glue will keep the pattern from shifting.

🐾 Note

Don't use adhesive tape to keep the pattern from shifting; it is difficult to remove from a mat after being inadvertently sliced by a rotary cutter.

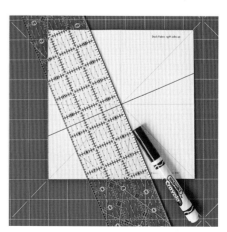

2 Extend both ends of the 2 bold pattern lines onto the mat about 2″ with a washable marker or chalk pencil.

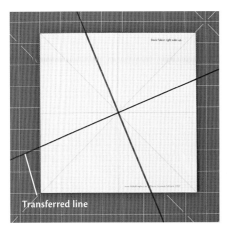

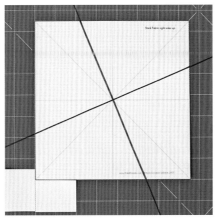

Transferred line

Lines transferred

Note

The four dashed lines—vertical, horizontal, and diagonal—on the pattern are never used for cutting but are useful to resize the pattern.

3 Make a bumper using 2 small stacks of sticky notes for perfect positioning of the pattern corner.

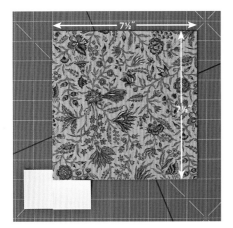

Tip

When you remove the sticky note bumper, mark the mat to locate that spot for the future.

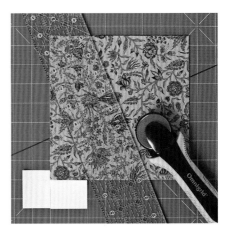

4 Replace the paper pattern and nest a stack of trimmed 7½″ squares, right sides up, as shown.

5 Align a ruler with both marked pattern lines on the mat, and cut the fabric squares.

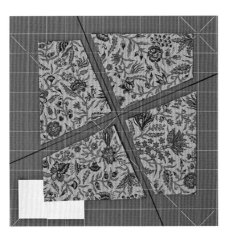

Perfect pieces galore (The bold cutting line has been extended inside the edges of the cut fabric squares for clarity.)

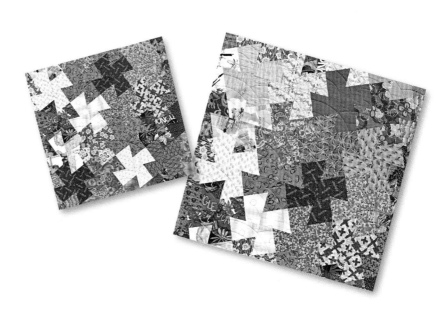

OPTION 2: TEMPLATE GUIDED CUTTING

1 Place a trimmed 7½" fabric square right side up anywhere on a mat.

2 Align a discarded paper template (or make a template), right side up, on the fabric square, matching corners. Cut the fabric guided by the template. The ruler will keep the paper in place.

This method comes in handy when you need to replace a fabric with another one or need to cut just a few pieces or are unable to mark a cutting mat.

Cutting Border Pieces

Border blocks can be cut and sewn more quickly using *double-size* pieces. Halving 1 square yields 2 *double-size* pieces.

> **🐚 Note**
>
> If you are cutting stacks of border pieces, make sure the fabrics are all right side up and maintain the same print direction. Corner border blocks are cut as single-size pieces (cut 4 to a square).

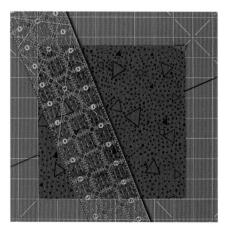

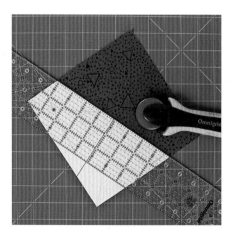

Method 1. Cut a fabric square in half along the guideline drawn on the mat (see pages 60–61). Squares may be stacked.

A pair of border pieces, sufficient for 2 blocks

Method 2. Use a paper template to cut 1 or 2 border pieces (see above). This method is also useful for scraps that are large enough to yield only 1 double-size piece.

✂ Note

Border pieces *must* be sewn as part of the complete square blocks when assembling the quilt top. It would be a nightmare to try to add them alone. (On the following two illustrations, single border pieces are colored in such a way as to differentiate them.)

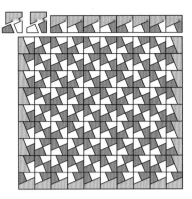

Pieced outer border: Each of 4 border corner blocks always includes 1 single and 1 double border piece.

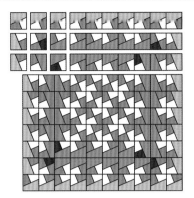

Pieced inner and outer borders: The *Santa Fe Windmill* quilt (page 64) has inner and outer borders abstracted from this illustration.

Jungle Windmill, made by Robin Strauss, Brooklyn, New York; quilted by Janice E. Petre, Sinking Spring, Pennsylvania; 2009, 60½″ square

Tahitian Sunset, made by Renée Kane Fields, Astoria, New York; quilted by Christine Frederick Janove, Brooklyn, New York; 2009, 48½″ × 60½″

The trial of the No-Waste Windmill; Constance Benson, Ethel McCall, and Frances Jackson, Riverbank State Park, New York, New York, 2005

Flannel Windmill, made by author; quilted by Janice E. Petre, Sinking Spring, Pennsylvania; 2009, 54½″ square

Made of 10½″ (trim size) squares of fabric

Santa Fe Windmill, made by Judith Hoffman Corwin, New York, New York; quilted by Janice E. Petre, Sinking Spring, Pennsylvania; 2009, 60½″ square

Key West Beauty, made by author; quilted by Janice E. Petre, Sinking Spring, Pennsylvania; 2003, 30½″ square

This quilt was featured in Times Square on Panasonic's 28′ × 38′ Astrovision screen. The sequence ran four times each hour during the fall 2009 holiday season and was presented by The City Quilter.

Detail of Key West Beauty

In 2001, I designed the unique folded foundation patterns for my book *Make It Simpler Paper Piecing*. One pattern was the Key West Beauty block. A few years later, I noticed what seems obvious now: Windmill pieces seem to appear within the lines of the Key West Beauty. I visualized a fabric square cut into four windmill pieces *with only two rotary cuts* and no leftover fabric.

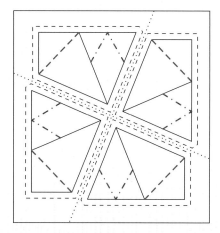

Key West Beauty pattern from *Make It Simpler Paper Piecing*, mirrored for paper foundation piecing

This method evolved from 6″ charm squares that I collected from online swaps in the early 1990s. I saved them in their envelopes, postmarked from around the United States, and petted the fabric from time to time. I wanted to make a Square-on-Point quilt from them but didn't know how to do so without wasting parts of the charms.

After developing the cutting technique for Old Italian Block (pages 49–54), I visited my charm drawer and thought there must be a way to cut those squares efficiently for Squares-on-Point. To make a long story short, I wrestled with the challenge for a day and came up with a method and formula by working with paper samples generated from Electric Quilt software. I have since refined the technique and the pattern into a versatile cutting pattern *and* top-piecing foundation.

Yardage calculations are easy. Two squares of fabric yield the equivalent of two blocks.

The original cutting pattern for *Square-on-Point* (seen on *Simply Quilts*) called for 8″ squares of fabric and yielded finished blocks of 6¾″. This pattern is available by download from www.makeitsimpler.com.

Square-on-Point (seen on *Simply Quilts*), made by author; quilted by Janice E. Petre, Sinking Spring, Pennsylvania; 2004–2009, 47¾″ square

Made to accompany the very first demonstration of the Make It Simpler Square-on-Point block, which debuted on the HGTV show *Simply Quilts*.

Making the Blocks

Rough-cut fabric square: 7¾″ minimum

Fabric square trim size: 7¼″ square

Unfinished block size: 6½″ square

Finished block size: 6″ square

CUTTING

To create the pieces for this block, cut through the lines of a paper pattern laid on top of fabric squares.

Photocopy the Square-on-Point Cutting Pattern on page 102; roughly trim the margin to ¼″.

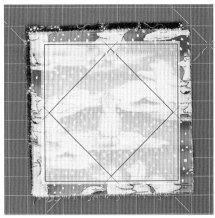

1 Prepare a stack of starched and pressed *rough-cut* (page 97) 7¾" fabric squares (minimum size); right sides up is preferable but not essential for this pattern. Lightly glue the cutting pattern to the top fabric square on the stack. Using Simple Foundations Translucent Vellum Paper (C&T Publishing) instead of opaque paper facilitates previewing motifs of the fabric.

☙ Note

In the Step 1 photo, the square is on point and the motif retains its orientation. Should the center square for this block be cut separately from a scrap or yardage, once turned on point, the motif would appear sideways. Cutting the center square on point to begin with would be wasteful, resulting in an awkward, bias-edged, square-on-point hole in the leftover yardage.

☙ Note

Since the pattern is symmetrical, it doesn't matter if the fabric squares and the pattern are right sides or wrong sides up. However, if the top fabric square is wrong side up, it won't pick up any glue residue. By keeping the remaining squares right sides up, cut patches needn't be organized right sides up after cutting.

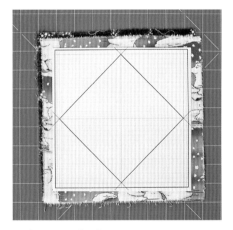

In this example, the pattern was photocopied onto an opaque paper, Carol Doak's Foundation Paper (C&T Publishing).

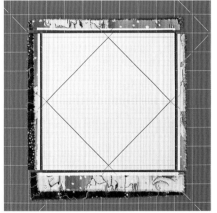

2 Cut the stack through the bold outside lines for an accurately cut 7¼" square stack.

3 Line up the ruler with any 1 of the 4 bold diagonal lines. Cut the stack along the ruler's edge completely from one edge of the paper to the other. Repeat to make 4 cuts. Do not disturb the stack.

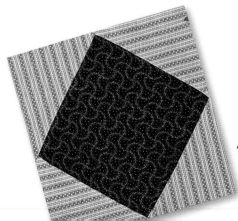

Author's vintage quilt block

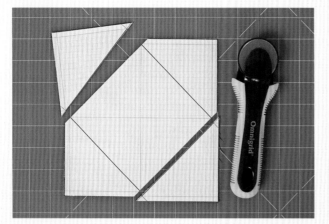

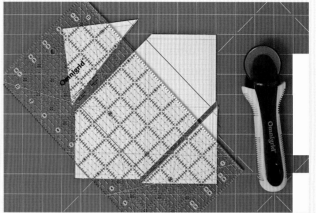

When the stack is disturbed…

…the cutting lines won't be continuous. Put everything back in order.

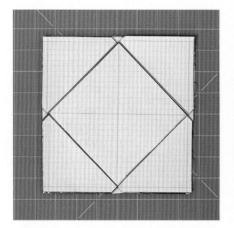

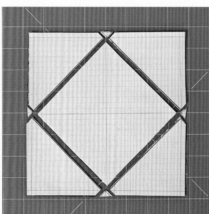

All 4 diagonals were cut through the lines.

Now the stack may be disturbed. The tiny triangles are the *only* waste.

Remove the center piece of paper. *Ah…*

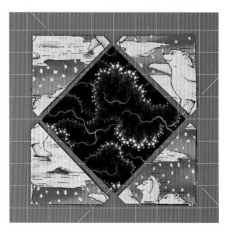

4 Remove the remaining pieces of paper. …*Ha!*

Removing layers reveals more patches; their unnecessary tips have been trimmed off in the process. The center square has bias edges. Two different fabric squares yield pieces for 2 interchangeable blocks in the manner of "robbing Peter to pay Paul." Of course, they may be swapped with other pieces.

SEWING THE BLOCK

OPTION 1: TRADITIONAL PIECING

Sew the triangles to the center square, referring to the instructions below for the sewing order.

OPTION 2: TOP FOUNDATION PIECING

Sewing this block together is straightforward and, for some, a piece of cake. For others it's problematic, with blame resting on a sewing machine or fabric. As a remedy, top paper piecing, a form of foundation piecing, is a classic solution.

Author's vintage quilt block

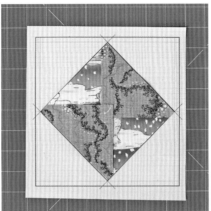
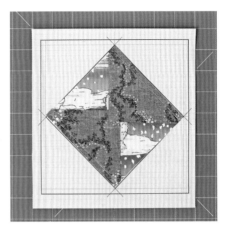

1 Lightly glue a center square right side up within its original footprint on a trimmed photocopy. Yes, this is something a child could do, which makes this suitable for involving children at home or school.

2 Position a pair of triangles, right side down, opposite each other just inside the printed diagonal line.

3 Sew ¼" in from the *printed line.* Shorten the stitch length to ease removing the paper *after* the top is assembled.

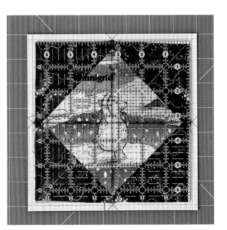

4 Press the triangles open. Use a dry iron or an iron without water in the reservoir. Steam could shrink the paper.

5 Repeat Steps 2–4 with 2 remaining triangles to complete the block.

6 Make a true-up square by marking a 6½" acrylic square into fourths with a permanent marker. Center it over the pieced block as shown, and trim any excess paper and fabric.

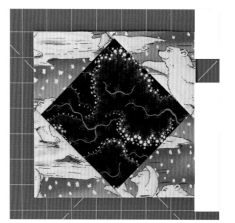

Back of trimmed block   Finished blocks

> ## ⚜ Tip
>
> There are two reasons to not remove the paper until after the blocks have been sewn together. The paper will stabilize blocks as they are sewn together; and if the fabric doesn't reach the edge of the block, leaving the paper in place provides an accurate guide for sewing.

Tips and Techniques
SEWING BIAS EDGES

Photo by Jeanne C. Delpit, Bernina of America

During machine sewing, the fabric sits on top of feed dogs, which move it along. These feed dogs are in contact only with the bottom layer of fabric. The top layer of fabric gets a piggyback ride and doesn't always move in sync with the bottom layer. If the bottom layer is on the bias, it will stretch. Some machines counter this problem. This is my counter-measure: To sew bias and straight-of-grain fabrics together, put the straight of grain on the bottom when possible. This applies to Arrowhead and Pineapple blocks as well.

When sewing two bias edges together, I have a *stop and start* tactic: Begin with my usual backstitch ¼″ in from the edge of the piece. Sink the needle and sew backward, stopping at the edge or thereabouts. Now sew forward. At most there will be two needle passes over the same area, not the usual three, and the edge of the fabric won't be drawn below the sewing bed.

Continue sewing but stop about halfway. Turn the unit over, and repeat, sewing until just beyond where you left off. This locks both edges, preventing them from stretching beyond their mate. Repeat this for the opposite triangle before stopping to press. The sewing sequence is variable. You may sew both sides halfway before turning the unit over.

I also *stop and start* when joining large nonbias blocks together to avoid pinning. On the final approach to the center, should there be a gap between the layers, ease in the gap by shortening the stitch length and by placing the gap side against the feed dogs.

DRAFTING A DIFFERENT SIZE CUTTING/ TOP-PIECING PATTERN

You'll need a sheet of ¼″ graph paper at least as large as the size of the pattern that you want.

Determine *what finished size block you want* or *what size fabric squares you want to use.* With the finished block size in mind, add 1¼″ to that number for the pattern size. For instance, the 7¼″ square pattern on page 102 makes a 6″ square finished block. A 9¼″ square pattern would make an 8″ square finished block. A 4¼″ square pattern would make a 3″ square finished block.

Otherwise, work from a rough-cut stack of starched fabric. Decide what size it will reasonably trim down to. That trim size is the pattern size. The finished block is 1¼″ less than this size.

Tip

Precut fabric squares are considered rough-cut fabric squares and should be spray starched and pressed with a hot iron before stacking to allow for their likely shrinkage.

1 Draw a square the size you want the pattern. For the pattern on page 102, I drew a 7¼″ square.

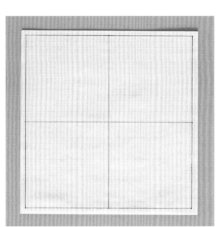

2 Draw perpendicular lines to divide the square into quarters.

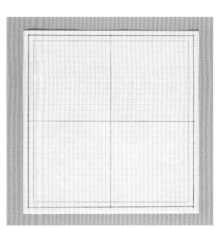

3 Draw parallel lines ¼″ inside each side of the square.

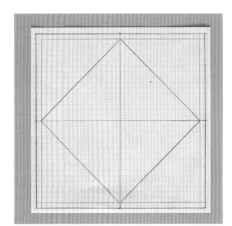

4 Draw a square on point by connecting the points where the perpendicular lines meet at the middle of each side of the inside square.

Note

Four colored pencils were used for illustration purposes. A single pencil would suffice.

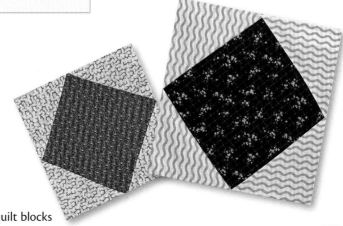

Author's vintage quilt blocks

THE FUDGE FACTOR

There must be a ¼″ seam allowance between each tip of the center square and the edge of the block. If not, when blocks are sewn together, these tips will appear chopped off; so it's essential the triangles be sewn to the square with a ¼″ seam.

Using Traditional Piecing methods (page 69), if an unfinished sample block measures less than 6½″, don't attempt a fix by sewing the triangles with less than a ¼″ seam. Try this to compensate: When cutting through the stack, instead of cutting exactly through the diagonal lines, cut offline, less than ⅛″, toward the center of the block for slightly larger triangles. Should any tips or points become chopped off when the top is assembled, I suggest you enjoy your sewing just as it is.

TRIUMPH OVER FABRIC

Flimsy, knit, loosely woven, thin, or slippery fabrics can be troublesome during sewing. If starching is not solving the problem, back such fabrics with nonwoven iron-on fusible interfacing for support. Silk fabric isn't a candidate for starch, but stabilizing it with interfacing is helpful. Bear in mind that the needs of hand and machine sewers vary, and your choice of starch or stabilizing with interfacing will affect your ease of quilting.

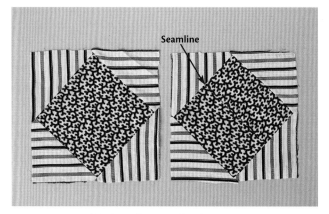

Square-on-Point blocks, collection of author, early twentieth-century.

Undersized pieces were joined in center square on right.

A Diamond Dance, by Didi Schiller, New York, New York, 2008, 81″ square

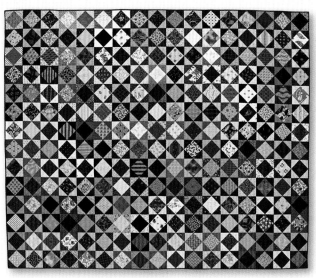

The Wedding Quilt, by author, 1996, 102½″ × 84½″

My first Square-on-Point quilt was made in 1996 with a method that called for 6½″ and 3½″ fabric squares. Pressing the seams open resulted in the flat appearance I desired.

PINEAPPLE BLOCK

Published in 1935, *The Romance of the Patchwork Quilt in America,* written by co-authors Carrie A. Hall and Rose G. Kretsinger, includes a Pineapple quilt that is captioned: "Made about 1870 by Hannah Ehlers… It is made entirely of wool and not quilted. Each piece in the block having a different shape, it required painstaking care in cutting and piecing to make so perfect a quilt…"

Now, nearly a century and a half later, pieces for Pineapple blocks can be cut efficiently, without waste, and easily, without measuring. Using disposable Make It Simpler Pineapple Cutting Patterns (page 103), 1 pattern, 2 pieces of fabric, and 14 contiguous rotary cuts yield the perfect 64 trapezoids and triangles for a pair of Pineapple blocks. Yardage calculations are easy: 2 rough-cut 16″ fabric squares plus 2 small center squares yield 2 finished 10″ square blocks. Their pieces are in opposite locations in the pair of blocks.

Any symmetrical Pineapple block pattern that calls for cutting standard-sized 2½″ center squares and 1½″-wide strips can use these cut pieces. However, these blocks are intended to be conventionally machine pieced, *not* foundation pieced.

Two-Color Pineapple, made by author; quilted by Janice E. Petre, Sinking Spring, Pennsylvania; 2007, 70½″ × 70½″

Unusually arranged in a half-drop setting, ordinary strongly contrasting fabrics make the quilt glow.

Making a Pair of Blocks

Rough-cut fabric square: 16″ minimum

Fabric square trim size: 15″

Fabric for 2½″ center squares

Unfinished block size: 10½″ square

Finished block size: 10″ square

CUTTING

To create the pieces for this block, cut on the lines of a paper pattern that is secured on top of the fabric. Follow the steps on pages 74–75 to make these blocks.

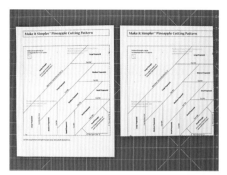

1 Tear or rough-cut (page 97) on the straight of grain, 2 starched pieces of fabric at least 16″ square. Fold each in half, right sides together, and then crosswise in half again into fourths. Press to crease the folds. Stack the folded fabric pieces.

Check the stack to be sure the folds are aligned along the bottom and right sides.

2 Photocopy the Make It Simpler Pineapple Cutting Pattern (page 103). Trim the 2 sides of the pattern along the *dashed* lines.

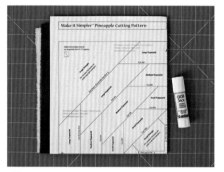

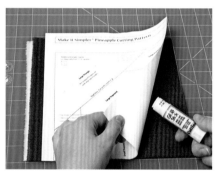

Warning

It is imperative that you trim and place the pattern *exactly* as noted in Steps 3 and 4 to achieve correctly cut block pieces.

3 Position the cutting pattern on the fabric stack, aligning its trimmed edges to the folded edges of the fabric.

4 Lightly glue the pattern to the top layer of fabric with 3 long strokes of a fabric or repositionable gluestick.

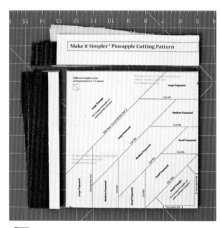

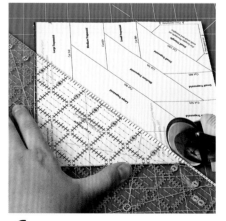

Tip

Push the rotary cutter blade down through all the layers at some point along the cutting line. Cut backward and forward to make the cut. This is easier than beginning the cut at the edge of the fabric.

5 Cut through both outside *solid* pattern lines to trim the raw fabric edges. The stack is now exactly 7½″ square. If unfolded, both fabrics would be 15″ square.

6 Cut along the first line at the base of the large triangle, through all layers, with a regular or large rotary cutter.

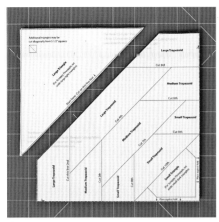

7 Slide the triangle stack aside.

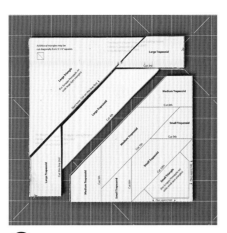

8 Make the second and subsequent cuts, moving the cut units aside.

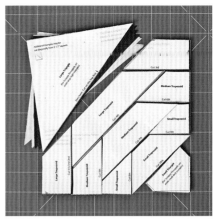

Finish cutting all pieces of the block. Eight layers of fabric have been cut.

Folded trapezoids result from the cuts on the folded fabric edges.

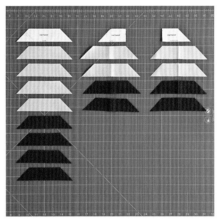

Pictured: 16 large trapezoids, 8 of which are cut folded. Also cut are a total of 16 medium and 16 small trapezoids, and 8 large and 8 small triangles. Remember to completely cut out the small triangles, as shown on the pattern. Total: 64 pieces cut, which is enough, with 2 added 2½″ squares, for 2 complete blocks.

9 Cut 1 square 2½″ from each fabric to be used in the center of each block (see pages 76–77).

 Tip

The paper pieces can be thrown away. If needed, one can be retrieved for use as a template. If a trapezoid is missing, look for it in the wastebasket. It's probably glued to a piece of paper. If it's not there, cut a new one with a paper template, and then the missing one will likely appear.

Tip

Unfold the pieces and store by size, regardless of color.

Organizing options

Note

Don't spend time neatly arranging the pieces; gaps between pieces are expected. The mock-up (page 76) is a checkpoint for the layout. It doesn't matter where bias or straight-of-grain trapezoids are placed. They are interchangeable.

If the sheet of freezer paper curls up and won't lie flat, secure its corners. Don't use tape; it could melt if touched by a hot iron. Instead, iron a strip (1″ wide or so) of freezer paper, shiny side down, diagonally across each corner to anchor them to the ironing surface.

Never iron on top of a rotary mat.

MAKING A MOCK-UP

Make a mock-up of both blocks. It's the only way to be certain every piece is used and positioned correctly. If there is time to sew only one block before being interrupted, it is easy to resume later. Cut two pieces of freezer paper, at least 16″ square. If a roll is under 18″ wide, overlap two smaller freezer paper pieces, and bond them together with the heat of an iron; protect the ironing surface with parchment paper placed on the shiny side of the freezer paper.

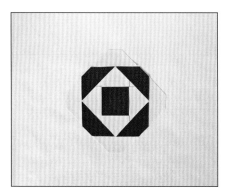

1 Lay a sheet of freezer paper, shiny side up, on an ironing surface. Place the darker of the 2 squares, right side up, in the center of the freezer paper, parallel to the edges of the paper, not on point. Frame the square with the small light triangles. Frame these triangles with 4 small dark trapezoids. Follow with the 4 light small trapezoids. Keep the right side up for all fabric pieces. Expect 8 "leftover" small trapezoids: 4 dark and 4 light. They are for the second block.

2 Add 4 dark medium trapezoids, followed by 4 light medium trapezoids.

3 Add 4 dark large trapezoids, then 4 light large trapezoids, and the 4 dark large triangles. If it doesn't look like this, the center square may be on point instead of parallel to the paper's edges or a trapezoid may be in the wrong place. There are leftover pieces because enough were cut for 2 blocks.

4 Make a mock-up of the second block from the remaining pieces. If a trapezoid of a particular size is missing, look for it in the first mock-up. Maybe there are 2 layers of fabric in one of the locations. When viewed, 1 mock-up has dark wings, resembling an X with ends in the corners of the large outside triangles, and the other has light wings.

5 Working from the center out, slowly fuse the freezer paper to the fabric pieces. Protect the iron with parchment paper.

SEWING A BLOCK

Press seams away from the center. Use ¼″ seam allowances.

Cutting the Pineapple block pieces this way is easy, but the sewing is traditional: a lot of straight-line sewing—but worth it.

> ## Tip
> Reduce stretching of the bias edges of the pieces. To sew the bias to the straight, sew with the bias on top and the straight of grain on the feed dogs. Any trapezoid, regardless of how it is cut from fabric, will always have two bias sides and two straight-of-grain sides.

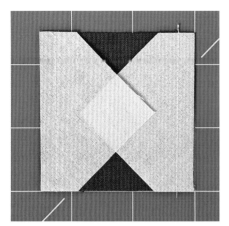

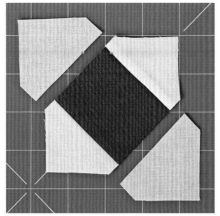

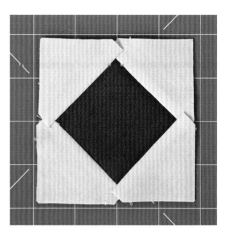

1 Lift the dark center square and 2 small triangles from the freezer paper. With right sides together, sew the triangles to opposite sides of the square. Press.

2 Sew the 2 remaining triangles to the unit and press. These triangles are considered Round #1. The final (eighth) round is the large corner triangles.

Round #1 complete

Note

This Square-on-Point unit should measure 3⅜" square, with its center measuring 2" square. If the unit is too large, merely shaving the unit to 3⅜" without regard to preserving the ¼" seam allowance around the outside edges isn't good enough. This is the time to attempt to set the Pineapple on the right course. Be flexible in your expectations and know that Pineapple construction embraces give and take.

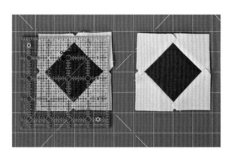

3 True up with an acrylic ruler, 4½" square or larger, that has been marked with guidelines traced from the Pineapple Center True-Up Guide (page 106).

Make It Simpler®
Pineapple Center
True-Up Guide

Pineapple Center True-Up Guide (pattern on page 106). A very slick trick for foundation piecers: Use the True-Up Guide as a paper piecing pattern!

Tip

An alternative to marking an acrylic ruler is to trace or photocopy the True-Up Guide (page 106) onto Simple Foundations Translucent Vellum Paper (C&T Publishing). Inexpensively laminate the copy on both sides with clear shipping tape before cutting out the vellum guide. Or, trace the guide onto see-through plastic template material. In any case, position the homemade guide on the Square-on-Point unit, draw the cutting lines, remove the guide, and then cut away the triangle excess using a ruler as a straight edge. Don't rotary cut against either of these homemade guides or you will shave off some of them.

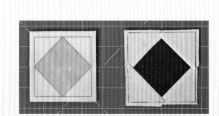

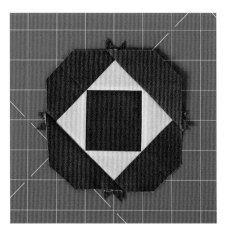

4 Sew a pair of dark small trapezoids to opposite sides of the unit, press, and add another pair of dark trapezoids to complete Round #2; press.

⚙ Note

To true up the unit, the center square should align with a 4½″ square ruler's gridlines. Check for the ¼″ seam allowance around the edges of the unit. The small triangles are now finished and should measure 1″ wide; the entire unit should be 4½″ square. If the unit is smaller than it should be, compensate by sewing the next round with a scant seam allowance or by offsetting a trapezoid when sewing it. A Pineapple isn't about perfect points. It's about a dazzling arrangement of 45-degree angles.

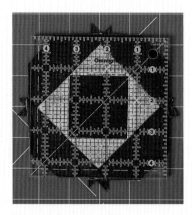

Use a 4½″ square ruler.

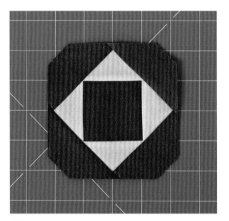

5 True up the unit so it measures 4½″ square.

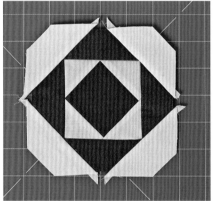

6 Sew Round #3. The block will progress quickly now as the trapezoids are added. Gaps between trapezoids occur from this round forward. The trapezoids, originally cut 1½″ wide, should now measure 1¼″ before and after the white trapezoids are trimmed.

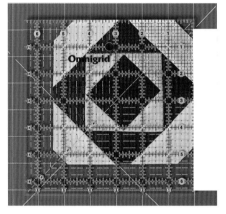

7 True up the unit. The current size of the block should be 5⅜″ square. Note the center square is *on point* for this measurement. Also note that the red trapezoid on the bottom happens to be skimpy; it's just less than 1¼″ wide. When it's time to add a medium red trapezoid, the trapezoid will be aligned against the edges of the adjacent white trapezoids and the standard ¼″ seam allowance taken, rather than aligning the new trapezoid to the skimpy edge.

The Make It Simpler Pineapple Trimming Guide (page 80) charts a block's dimensions as rounds are added. If the block is skimpy, either offset the pieces or adjust the seam allowance as a course correction. *Notice the block's center square is on point only when the overall block measurement is in eighths, not halves.* If you check the dimensions of a block in progress and it appears to be way oversized, put down the rotary cutter. You've probably rotated the block by accident and are reading the guide incorrectly. Trueing up as you sew should be sufficient. The guide is only a growth chart. The idea behind it is to monitor the block as it grows to 10½″ square, unfinished, without any surprises.

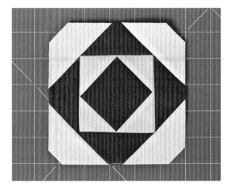

Trued-up unit measures 5⅜″ square.

8 Sew and true up Round #4 so it measures 6½″ square.

9 Sew and true up Round #5 so it measures 7⅜″ square.

10 Sew and true up Round #6 so it measures 8½″ square.

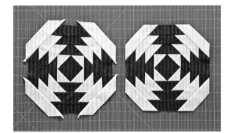

11 Sew and true up Round #7 so it measures 9⅜″ square.

12 Sew and true up Round #8 so it measures 10½″ square.

Leftover trimmings from a block are modest.

Repeat Steps 1–12, alternating placement of red and white pieces, to make the companion block.

🦋 **Tip**

When your cutting area is small, cut *starched, folded,* and pressed fabric strips into squares. A 2½″ square ruler works well as a template.

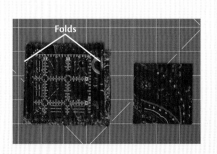

Folds

Round 1
Small triangles
Measures: 3⅜" square

Round 2
Small trapezoids
Measures: 4½" square

Round 3
Small trapezoids
Measures: 5⅜" square

In Rounds 2 and 3, the small trapezoids have the same footprint.

Round 4
Medium trapezoids
Measures: 6½" square

Round 5
Medium trapezoids
Measures: 7⅜" square

In Rounds 4 and 5, the medium trapezoids have the same footprint.

Round 6
Large trapezoids
Measures: 8½" square

Round 7
Large trapezoids
Measures: 9⅜" square

In Rounds 6 and 7, the large trapezoids have the same footprint.

Round 8
Large triangles
Measures: 10½" square

✄ Notes

■ Illustrations are drawn for clarity without outside edge seam allowances.

■ All measurements include the outside edge ¼" seam allowances. The odd Rounds measurements end in ⅜" increments; while the even Rounds measurements end in ½" increments.

■ Measure top to bottom or side to side.

Pineapple Block Design Ideas

LIGHT- AND DARK-WINGED BLOCKS

My Pineapple blocks are considered either light-winged or dark-winged, depending on whether the corner triangles are of the lighter or darker fabric.

If you need more of one block than the other for your quilt design, you can easily *convert* a light-winged block into a dark-winged block, or vice versa.

Light-winged block   Dark-winged block

The light and dark trapezoids in pairs of successive rounds—2 and 3, 4 and 5, 6 and 7—have the *identical* footprint. So, changing a light-winged block to a dark-winged block, or vice versa, is easy. After the pieces are cut and mocked up using the instructions on pages 73–76, follow the instructions below.

From light-winged to dark-winged:

1. Cut a new 2½″ dark center square.

2. Cut 4 new small light triangles (from leftover large light triangles) to replace discarded small dark triangles.

3. Switch the position of the pairs of light and dark trapezoids.

4. Cut 4 new large dark triangles to replace the large light triangles.

From dark-winged to light-winged:

1. Cut a new 2½″ light center square.

2. Cut 4 new small dark triangles (from leftover large dark triangles) to replace discarded small light triangles.

3. Switch the position of the pairs of light and dark trapezoids.

4. Cut 4 new large light triangles to replace the large dark triangles.

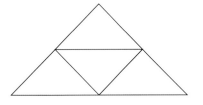   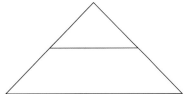

Cut 4 small triangles from 1 large triangle.   Or, cut 1 small triangle and 1 trapezoid from 1 large triangle (if needed, depending on your chosen quilt design).

THE HALF-DROP SETTING

When it came time to sew the blocks together in *Two-Color Pineapple*, I was troubled by a drawback. The technique made economic sense. It yielded one light- and one dark-winged block efficiently from two squares of fabric. But setting the blocks in a horizontal layout wouldn't be as dramatic a design as using *only* light- or dark-winged blocks. So, I arranged the blocks in an unusual half-drop setting. I don't recall ever seeing a half-drop Pineapple layout, probably because the likelihood of someone deliberately making a pile of matching light and dark blocks was remote.

Two-Color Pineapple (detail), by author (full quilt on page 73). Triangular shape forms at the intersection of 3 blocks because of solid-color fabric. Solid-color fabrics disguise seamlines, creating large triangular-shaped forms.

ELONGATED BLOCKS

Rather than piecing half-blocks to complete this setting, I made four elongated dark-winged blocks and cut them in half to make eight half-sized blocks.

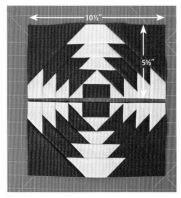

1 Make 4 dark-winged blocks following the instructions (pages 73–79), with the exception of the large light trapezoids in Round 7. Instead, cut 2 large light trapezoids, at least 2″ wide, from 2 leftover large light triangles. Substitute them for 2 opposing large light trapezoids in each block. True-up the unfinished block to 10½″ × 11″. Stabilize an elongated block's 10½″ center width with a 1¼″–2″-wide strip of fusible interfacing.

2 Cut the elongated block through the center through the 10½″ width.

3 Each half block is 10½″ × 5½″. Note that when the half block is inserted at the top and bottom of the columns, the tips of the trapezoids are "lost" next to the binding; but in the scheme of things, it really is not noticeable.

Layout for *Two-Color Pineapple* (page 81): There are 21 each dark- and light-winged blocks; 4 elongated dark-winged blocks, each cut in half; and 3 light-winged blocks converted to 3 dark-winged blocks. The total is 49 blocks in all; 70″ square finished

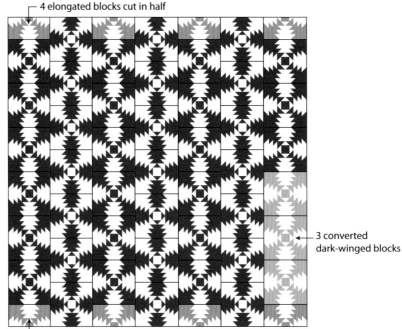

4 elongated blocks cut in half

3 converted dark-winged blocks

4 elongated blocks cut in half

I recommend using solid-colored fabrics. For the design to dominate, seams between blocks in vertical columns shouldn't be noticeable. I had 7 yards of each fabric on hand and cut into it a few blocks at a time. Though I didn't, I could have torn off 8″–10″-wide lengths, parallel to the selvage, from the dark fabric at the beginning and set it aside for binding. I prefer Robert Kaufman brand Kona Cotton solid fabric for many reasons, including the consistency of its dye lots. Should you judiciously purchase fabric for only a few blocks and need more, it will usually be available.

> ## 🔹 Note
> The pattern requires a minimum 16″ fabric square (rough-cut fabric square) for every full-size block. But undersized pieces may be first sewn together before folding and trimming.

SETTING TRIANGLE BLOCKS

In *Scrappy Pineapple*, the scrappy blocks are all dark winged (page 81). Set in an on-point layout, a pattern of light-colored circles forms. Unfortunately, this layout requires piecing corner- and side-setting triangles. I absolutely didn't want to piece triangles once I'd cut sets of 64 pieces so quickly. Instead I cut ready-made Pineapple blocks in half diagonally into triangles, after stabilizing the diagonals with interfacing. As for losing the ¼″ seam allowance along the sides of the quilt, I didn't think it would be noticeable. I've noticed this practiced on nineteenth-century quilts.

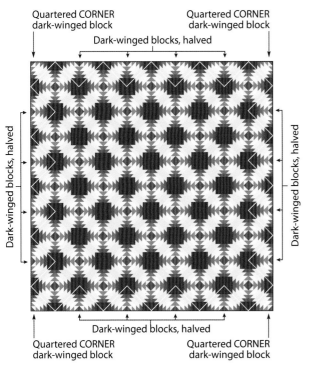

Quartered CORNER dark-winged block   Quartered CORNER dark-winged block

Dark-winged blocks, halved

Dark-winged blocks, halved

Dark-winged blocks, halved

Dark-winged blocks, halved

Quartered CORNER dark-winged block   Quartered CORNER dark-winged block

Layout for *Scrappy Pineapple:* There are 41 dark-winged blocks plus 8 dark-winged blocks, halved, for the side triangles; and 1 enlarged dark-winged block, quartered, for the corners. The total is 49 blocks in all; 70″ square finished.

Scrappy Pineapple, made by author; quilted by Janice E. Petre, Sinking Spring, Pennsylvania; 2007, 74″ square

SIDE SETTING TRIANGLES

1 Select 8 dark-winged blocks, each 10½" square, unfinished (page 81).

2 Fuse a 1¼"–2"-wide strip of fusible interfacing diagonally across the wrong side of the block. Trim the interfacing flush with the block's corners.

3 Cut the block in half diagonally through the interfacing strip.

One block equals 2 side triangles.

CORNER TRIANGLES

> ### 🐾 Note
>
> Making things Simpler meant not piecing 4 corner triangles. My unconventional solution? I enlarged 1 block, replacing Round #7 trapezoids with 2"-wide pieces and quartered the block diagonally. This didn't detract from the overall look of the quilt.

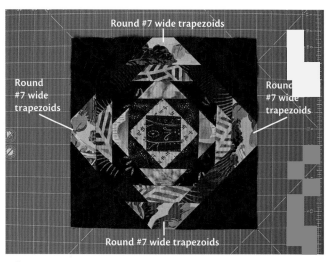

Round #7 wide trapezoids

Round #7 wide trapezoids

Round #7 wide trapezoids

Round #7 wide trapezoids

1 Block enlarged to 11½" square, unfinished, by wide trapezoids at the edges (see Note on the left).

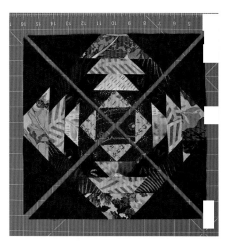

2 Fuse 2 strips of interfacing, 1¼"–2" wide, diagonally across the wrong side of the block, trimming the corners.

3 Cut the block in half diagonally in both directions.

One enlarged block equals 4 unconventional corner triangles.

TROPICAL PINEAPPLE BORDER

Tropical Pineapple, made by author; quilted by Janice E. Petre, Sinking Spring, Pennsylvania; 2009, 38″ square

A mock-up of brightly colored solids alternating with dark gray and black wings

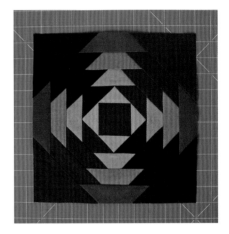

One square of lime green fabric, when cut, yields 24 trapezoids, enough to spread out through several blocks. Since this quilt used only *dark* large triangles, leftover large lime triangles could have been cut down and used as additional trapezoids and small triangles.

Making the Border Block

Fabric: Leftover scraps from quilt construction
Unfinished border block size: 4½″ × 10½″
Finished border block size: 4″ × 10″
Simple Foundations Translucent Vellum (C&T Publishing)

The borders complement the shapes in my *Tropical Pineapple* quilt and are for paper piecing. Use templates (page 105) to cut the fabric pieces; paper piece the blocks. The foundation pattern is on page 104; it is reversed for paper piecing.

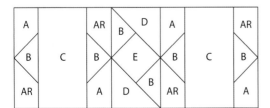

Border block schematic for piece placement

My unique construction method, the subject of my previous two books, results in automatically aligned points in each sewn block. Instead of piecing several subunits and sewing them into a block, I sew the block entirely on one pattern sheet that has been folded, accordion-style, prior to piecing. The folds result in perfectly aligned seamlines. Once pieced, the paper is refolded and sewn through the printed seamlines without pins.

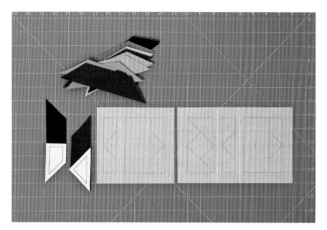

1 Scraps readied for piecing. The Pineapple Border pattern is too long to fit on a page. Two sections must be joined to prepare the pattern for piecing. Photocopy the pattern (page 104) twice onto sheets of Simple Foundations Translucent Vellum. Trim excess margins to roughly ¼″. Cut one copy along the *red* dotted line. Reserve section F; toss away section G.

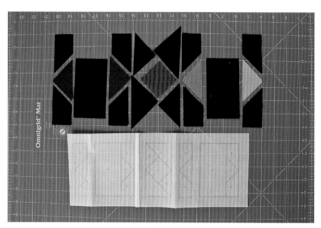

2 Join section F to the remaining pattern photocopy, using machine sewing rather than glue or ordinary tape. Tape will melt under the iron, and glue is unlikely to hold within the narrow area. Don't cut the pattern apart. Instead, crease by folding it, aligning the seamlines. The fold lines are dotted lines, the seamlines are solid lines. Make a mock-up of pieces to be sewn on the unprinted side of the foundation pattern.

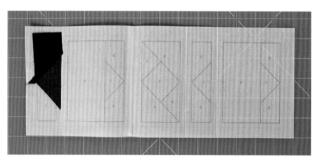

3 Sew 2 pieces in place after checking that they extend ¼″ beyond seamlines with printed side down.

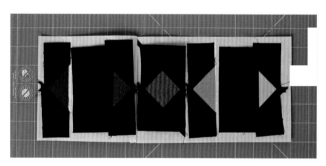

4 Sew all pieces in place.

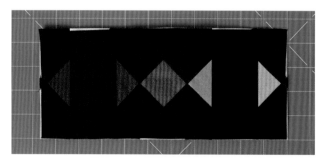

5 Unite the 4 subunits. Refold each, one at a time, and sew through the seamlines. Trim pattern to 4½″ × 10½″.

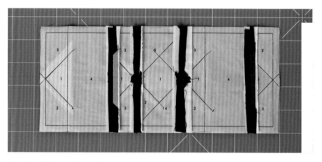

Back of sewn foundation

Why are tiny dots printed on the Pineapple Cutting Pattern's large triangles?

A: They are guides to divide each corner triangle into a trapezoid and small triangle, sometimes used in place of a large corner triangle.

Which is easiest of the three Pineapples to make?

A: The Two-Color Pineapple; there are only two fabrics to choose.

What are the implications of using directional fabric?

A: Some of the pieces will be cut on grain and others on bias. A square of striped fabric will yield pieces that look different because of diagonal and horizontal/vertical combinations.

Can the pieces be foundation pieced?

A: Because they are of standard cut sizes (2½″ centers, 1½″-wide trapezoids) they will fit most existing paper-pieced and preprinted muslin patterns. I have written two Make It Simpler books about paper piecing, yet I would *not* foundation piece Pineapples when I have precut pieces at hand. The back-and-forth trimming with scissors would be a royal nuisance.

Will the Pineapple Rule work with these pieces?

A: Yes, this popular ruler (available at www.possibilitiesquilt.com) corresponds to the Make It Simpler Pineapple Pattern.

How do I cut larger fabric squares?

A: To cut fabric squares larger than your ruler: Cut or tear a squarish piece of fabric larger than needed, fold it into quarters, and trim it to half (not a quarter) the size needed. For example, cut a 25″ square of fabric with 2 strokes by folding into quarters a minimum 26″ square of fabric. The folded fabric is roughly 13″ square. With a 12½″ square ruler, trim both raw edges. The unit measures 12½″ square and unfolds to 25″ square. The trick is also useful when a rotary mat is too small for a large fabric square.

Black and White Pineapples (detail), made by Phyllis Spalla, Tucson, Arizona; quilted by Nubin Jensen, 2008

Dark- and light-winged blocks set on point

Note

What could go wrong? Not stacking all the folded edges together, for one thing, or not placing the trimmed edge of the pattern on the folded sides of the fabric, for another. Both oversights would result in useless half-trapezoids instead of folded trapezoids. If needed, additional trapezoids can be made with 1½″ fabric strips and a discarded paper template, but it is usually more practical to cut another folded square.

Tip

Freezer paper mock-ups are advantageous. Prepare them when the opportunity exists and keep a stack of them ready to sew. Pieces fixed on freezer paper won't tumble off a design wall or fall out of order. Freezer paper may be reused. Flatten and store sheets of it underneath a rotary mat. When sewing a Pineapple, or any other block, mark "top" on the freezer paper if the direction matters.

Tip

Once familiar with the routine, work on a few blocks simultaneously. Add a round to each block, consecutively, in one sitting, before pressing the entire group. Likewise, when familiar making two-fabric blocks, forgo the freezer paper mock-ups.

In the early 1990s I began printing geometric block patterns with Electric Quilt software onto onion-skin paper suitable for foundation piecing. Sometime later *McCall's Quilting* magazine launched the Basic Realities contest, which featured Jinny Beyer fabric. Rising to the challenge of incorporating many fabrics into a quilt, I used one of my early patterns with success. It was karma that among the prizes I won were a half-dozen books from C&T Publishing. I made a miniature version in 2000 and then began *Self-Mitered Log Cabin*, having refined my block pattern to have every strip finish at the same width, eliminating the small, irregular triangles at the tips. The block has no bias edges and is simply sewn strip to strip. I follow the lines on paper for absolute accuracy, which results in perfectly matched self-made miters.

Self-Mitered Log Cabin, made by author; quilted by Janice E. Petre, Sinking Spring, Pennsylvania; 2002–2008, 69″ × 81″

Making the Blocks

Unfinished block size: 6½″ square

Finished block size: 6″ square

A block

B block

They look identical but they aren't. Examine the fabric strips at the bottom of the blocks; one is light, the other dark.

PREPARATION AND CUTTING

Make two photocopies of the pattern (page 107) onto Simple Foundations Translucent Vellum Paper or Carol Doak's Foundation Paper (C&T Publishing) for a pair of practice blocks. Trim the top and bottom margins to ½" beyond the dashed lines. Eventually a photocopy will be needed for each block in a quilt.

Cut assorted 8" × 1½" fabric strips from starched and pressed fabric. The strips may exceed 8" in length; any excess will be trimmed off during construction.

Two practice blocks require 16 different fabrics. Each pattern uses 8 different fabrics: pick 3 light, 2 medium, and 3 dark for each of these practice blocks.

Arrange each group of 8 from light to dark.

SEWING THE FOUNDATION

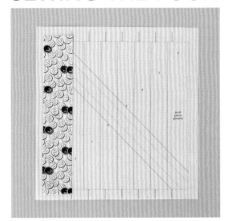

> ### 🦋 Tip
> For future blocks, streamline the process by stacking the first and second strips right sides together. Lightly glue the foundation and position the stack, with the lightest fabric wrong side down, in the #1 column.

1 Place pattern printed side down. With one group of 8 strips, glue the lightest color, right side up, to the #1 section of the foundation. Use a fabric or restickable gluestick. Note the positioning arrow heads at both ends.

2 Place the next strip, wrong side up, directly on top of the first strip.

> ### 🦋 Tip
> Set up the sewing machine with a #14 needle and a shorter-than-average stitch length. Use a neutral thread color in the bobbin. The shorter stitches perforate the paper for easy removal later. I use medium gray in the bobbin and cherry red in the spool. The red stitches are easy to see on the paper, won't show in the finished block, and are cheerful.

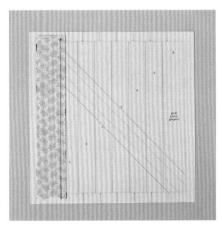

3 Holding the strips to the paper, or pin, turn the foundation over. Starting outside the dashed line, sew on the solid line between pieces 1 and 2.

Photo by Jeanne C. Delpit, Bernina of America

4 End stitching beyond the opposite dashed line. Backstitching is unnecessary; the paper will eventually be trimmed on the dashed line.

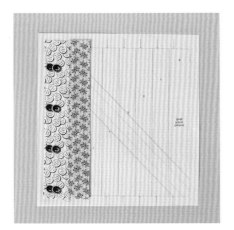

5 Open sewn strip and press.

> ✂ **Tip**
>
> Finger-pressing may be sufficient for starched fabric. If the fabric doesn't lie flat, press with an iron or lightly dab some glue on the fabric in the seam allowance. I prefer using a gluestick instead of pins. *When ironing, use a pressing cloth* if the foundation's lines smear; toner from some copiers is heat sensitive.

6 Secure the third strip, wrong side up, on top of the second strip, aligned with the arrows. Turn the block over and sew on the line between pieces 2 and 3.

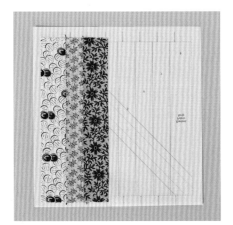

7 Open sewn strip and press.

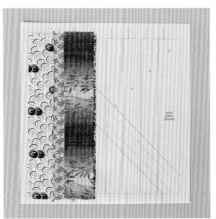

8 Secure the fourth strip, wrong side up on top of the third strip, aligned with the next arrows.

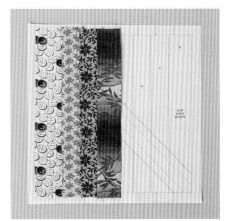

9 Turn the block over, and sew on the line between pieces 3 and 4. Open sewn strip and press.

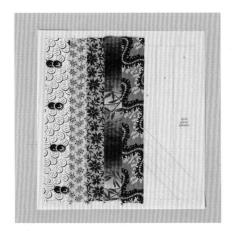

10 Repeat this process for the fifth strip.

11 Repeat this process for all 8 strips. Make the second block following the same process. Do not sew or baste around the edges. Press the blocks (no steam) to set the stitches.

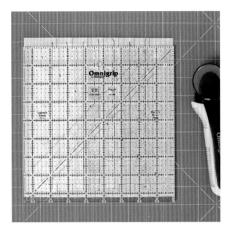

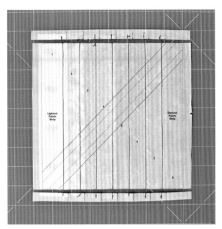

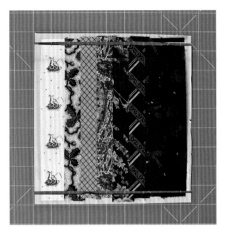

12 Trim 1 of the blocks 7½″ tall, preserving the dashed lines. Do not trim the sides.

Trimmed block (back)

Trimmed block (front)

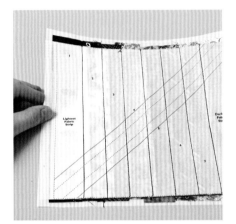

13 With the trimmed block on top, place the trimmed and untrimmed blocks right sides together, with the *lightest* fabric strip of 1 block facing the *darkest* fabric strip of the other block. Be sure the seams nest together.

Option 1 to check alignment: Roll the top block down (or up).

Option 2 to check alignment: Roll the top block across.

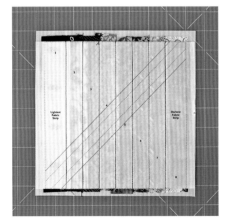

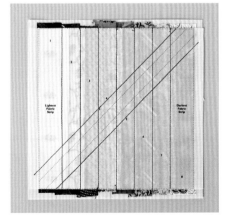

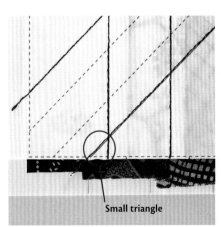

Small triangle

The block seams nest together. Again, the trimmed block is always on top.

14 Sew through both blocks, along the solid diagonal lines on the top sheet. Pins shouldn't be necessary. Ignore the diagonal lines on the back of the untrimmed sheet.

Note the small triangle (see Step 20, page 93).

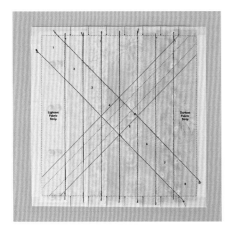

The backside: Again, ignore this side.

15 Lift back a flap for a peek at the chevron. Oh my gosh. You notice 14 strips, not 16.

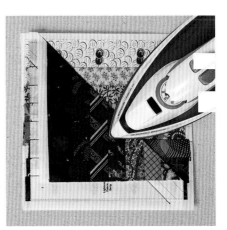

16 Press both diagonal seams.

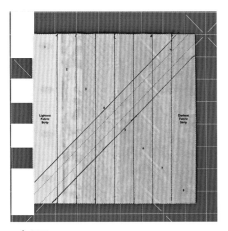

17 Fold the diagonal seams back to the original shape. Trim the sewn pair to 7½″ square. Preserve the perimeter dashed lines.

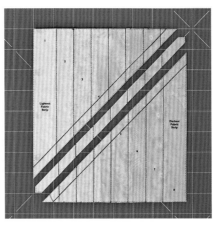

18 Cut through the sewn pair along the dashed diagonal lines.

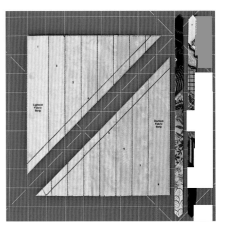

Two thin strips will be leftover.

A mound of leftover strips from a quilt top in progress

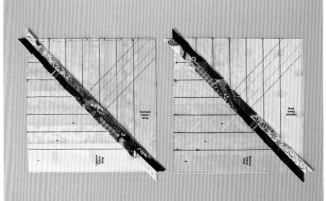

19 Open the blocks and press the seams open. Some dashed lines on the backs may seem out of place. This is not a mistake; they were on the backs and were ignored.

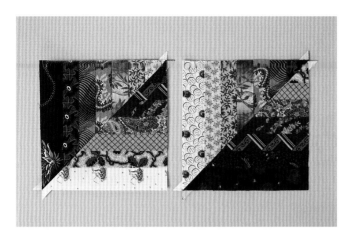

The blocks, front view, before trueing up

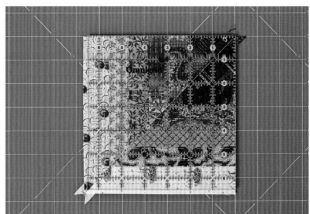

20 True up to 6½″ square. Align the 45° diagonal of the ruler on the block's diagonal seam. Preserve the ¼″ triangle square corner. The inside finished strips measure ⅞″ wide. The outer unfinished strips measure 1⅛″ wide because they include a ¼″ seam allowance.

The ¼″ triangle squares (circled) will disappear as the blocks are sewn together.

Follow the above procedure to make the quilt blocks. Sort the blocks into two groups: A blocks and B blocks. Quickly arrange all the A and B blocks to form a barn raising layout (page 94). Now rearrange the blocks to your satisfaction.

> ❧ **Note**
> Remove the paper patterns only after the top, including a border, if any, is assembled.

⚓ Note

There are subtleties to this block. It begins with eight strips, but ends with only seven, a result of the pattern compensating for loss in the diagonal seam allowance. Because of this nuance, the shortest strip in each block will finish at the same width as the other strips. *Reality Check* (page 95) had short strips that formed irregular triangles because I neglected the diagonal seam allowance. Because the lightest or darkest strip will disappear when a pair of A and B blocks are made, the blocks look original instead of halves of twin sets.

In this barn raising layout, the only seams that need to be matched are in the horizontal center row.

ASK ANITA:

May I use ordinary opaque paper instead of translucent vellum?

A: Yes, though using the vellum at least for the first few blocks will streamline the learning technique.

Is this a complicated pattern?

A: Absolutely not. It's suitable for anyone who knows how to rotary cut and machine sew, including beginners. It's a scrappy quilt suited for fabric collectors.

Why are there 14 arrow marks on the pattern?

A: They are my positioning markers for the fabric strips and are visible when vellum is used. When adding strips, instead of relying on the edge of the previously sewn strip as a guide, align successive strips at the arrows.

Must the strips be cut exactly to 8″ × 1½″?

A: It's helpful, otherwise large pieces and scraps may dominate the strip pile. Cutting a large print to size will reveal which areas of the print will appear in a strip.

Trimming an occasional oversize strip after it's been sewn to the block is possible but inefficient. Know that excessive seam allowances will make a quilt heavier from the unnecessary fabric.

Technically, a strip should be cut 1⅜″ wide. I add an extra ⅛″ and specify 1½″-wide fabric strips for two reasons: It's easier to cut 1½"-wide strips, and the ⅛" is for wiggle room, especially for the very lightest and darkest strips at either edge.

It's time-consuming to rummage through uncut yardage or scrap strips to make a block. To speed up the process, have a few hundred strips cut and available from which to pull groups of eight.

The initial strip of the eight that I select is usually a medium. I audition it over the strip pile to see what will work with it. I avoid my favorite fabric strips, reaching instead for one that seems ugly or garish or difficult to pair. I pick among the "difficult" strips first while there are plenty of favorites around to complement them. My dream is to incorporate as many different fabrics as possible into a quilt.

Why sew through paper?

A: The pattern lines on the paper enable sewing an absolutely straight line, guaranteeing the alignment for a perfect miter. Also, because paper is a stabilizer, the blocks will feed evenly through a sewing machine.

Fabric Tips

Accumulate fabric strips over time, sorting by color, not by dark or light value. Intermingling them by color alone readily distinguishes one print from another. Usually a print's background determines which color pile it belongs in. As new fabrics come your way, check the "strip pile" by color to see if a fabric has been previously cut.

My *Self-Mitered Log Cabin* (page 88) is 99 percent reproduction fabrics. The quilt is never going to become outdated. It was "old" before it was put together. I've also seen the block look striking in hip twenty-first-century fabrics.

Reality Check, by author, 1997, 37" square

GLOSSARY

by Marcella Peek

Marcella Peek fell in love with quilting fifteen years ago and has won several ribbons for her quilts. She taught quilting classes for eight years. Currently Marcella is serving on the boards of her local quilt guild and the Northern California Quilt Council.

Asymmetrical   A stripe or plaid patterned fabric that has an uneven arrangement of its design.

Design Wall   Viewing the piece straight on, like looking at artwork hung on a wall, allows the quilter to view the entire project and look at color balance and block placement. To do this, a design wall can be made from something as simple as pinning batting or a flannel sheet to a door or curtain rod or as permanent as covered rigid insulation board mounted to a wall. The critical issue is being able to view the project vertically.

Directional Fabric   Fabric with a print that has a definite direction or nap is called directional fabric. Care should be taken to ensure that stripes, characters, or animals point in the desired direction when pieced.

Fabric Prints   Designs on fabrics can be achieved by many methods. Some that are common to quilted fabrics are *printed*, where the design is printed onto one side of a plain base fabric; *woven*, where the dyed threads are woven into patterns; and *batik*, where wax is applied to portions of the plain base fabric and the dye only reacts with the uncoated fabric.

Fat Quarter   A quarter yard of fabric is 9″ by the width of the fabric. To make a "fat" quarter, fabric is cut twice as wide at 18″ by half the width of the fabric.

Finished Block   The final sewn size of a quilt block without added seam allowances.

Freezer Paper   A paper originally intended for wrapping meat that has a light coating of plastic on one side. It is often available at the supermarket or from the butcher. The coated side can be pressed to fabric with a hot iron and will adhere temporarily and leave no residue.

Freezer Paper for Mock-Ups   This is a great way to preview the completed block. Cut the pieces for a block, and iron them to a square of freezer paper. Changes can be made, without having to use a seam ripper, until the block is just as desired.

Iron, Dry   An iron without any steam holes on the soleplate. The absence of holes allows for smoother pressing and less distortion. Also, no water in the iron means no drips or spots on the fabric.

Miters   The corners of a block or quilt borders are joined with a 45-degree angle, like a picture frame.

Mock-up   To lay out all the pieces needed for a block in the proper final arrangement. This is great to do in preparation for sewing the block to ensure that all the pieces are assembled into their proper place.

Piece   The individual pieces that together make up a block.

Pieced   Perhaps the most common type of quilt; it is made by sewing together geometric pieces of fabric.

Right Side/Wrong Side   The right side of a fabric is the one that shows in the finished product, and the wrong side ends up on the inside.

Rough-Cut   Fabric cut larger than needed, often with raw edges. I starch and press it well before trimming it to the final accurate size. This allows for greater accuracy.

Scraps   Fabric pieces that are smaller than what is needed for a patch. Several scraps can be sewn together to make fabric large enough for a piece.

Stacked Squares   Oversized pieces of fabric that are stacked up and ready to be subcut.

Stitch Length   For sewing blocks together, it's important to find the balance between a strong seam and one whose stitches are long enough to use a seam ripper when necessary. Many quilters find that balance at a setting of 2.5, which measures about ten stitches per inch.

Straight of Grain   Fabric has three grains: lengthwise, crosswise, and bias. Lengthwise grain runs parallel to the finished edge of the fabric, and it is the most stable. Crosswise grain runs from one finished edge to the other and has a bit more stretch to it. Bias grain is at a 45-degree angle to the woven threads and has the most give to it.

Subunits   Pieced units or sections of a block that fit together to form a complete block.

Tearing Fabric   At times the yardage for a quilt is so large that it is unwieldy to work with. To tear the yardage into smaller, more manageable pieces, use scissors to clip the edge, grasp the fabric on either side of the clip, and tear the fabric into two pieces.

Triangle Half-Square Units   Two right triangles that fit together to form a square.

Triangle Quarter-Square Units   Four right triangles that fit together to make a square.

Trim Size   The exact dimensions to cut a stack of over-sized pieces of fabric.

True Up   To check the dimensions of a sewn subunit, block in progress, or unfinished block and, when necessary, to trim the unit to its accurate measurement. Trimming a block to size implies shaving down one or two sides. Trueing up involves three variables: maintaining the ¼″ outside seam allowances, ascertaining the size and position of the inside subunit(s), and maintaining the correct block size.

Unfinished Block   A quilt block that has not been set into the finished project. The block still has its added outer seam allowances.

Yardage   The amount of each fabric needed for a project. The larger pieces of fabric are then cut into strips or other shapes for making blocks.

Make It Simpler® 7″ No Patience Window Frame Template Guide for a 9″ Finished Block

© Anita Grossman Solomon 2009   www.MakeItSimpler.com

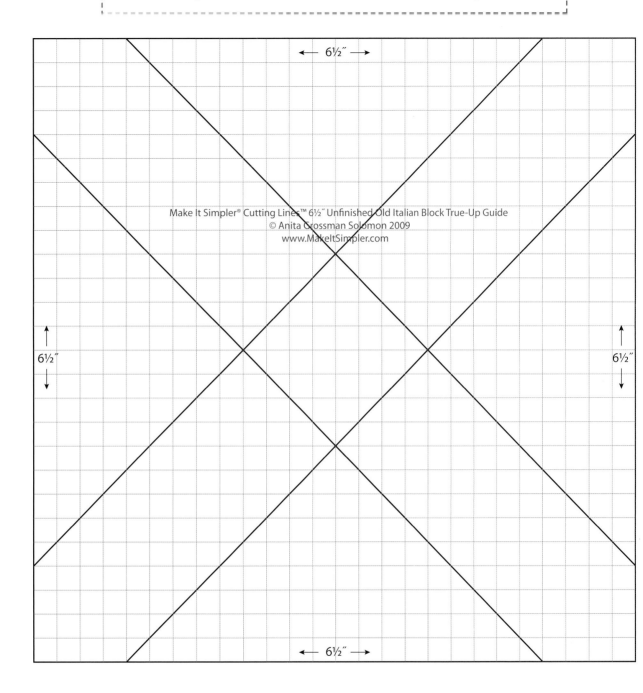

Make It Simpler® Cutting Lines™ 6½˝ Unfinished Old Italian Block True-Up Guide
© Anita Grossman Solomon 2009
www.MakeItSimpler.com

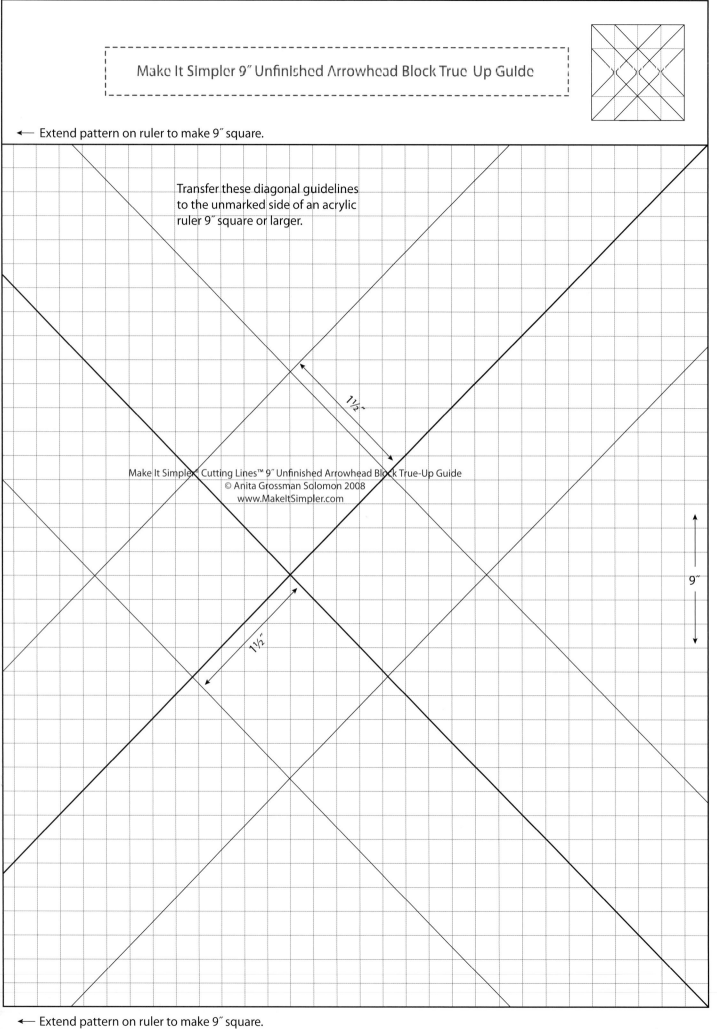

Make It Simpler 9″ Unfinished Arrowhead Block True Up Guide

← Extend pattern on ruler to make 9″ square.

Transfer these diagonal guidelines
to the unmarked side of an acrylic
ruler 9″ square or larger.

1½″

Make It Simpler® Cutting Lines™ 9″ Unfinished Arrowhead Block True-Up Guide
© Anita Grossman Solomon 2008
www.MakeItSimpler.com

1½″

9″

← Extend pattern on ruler to make 9″ square.

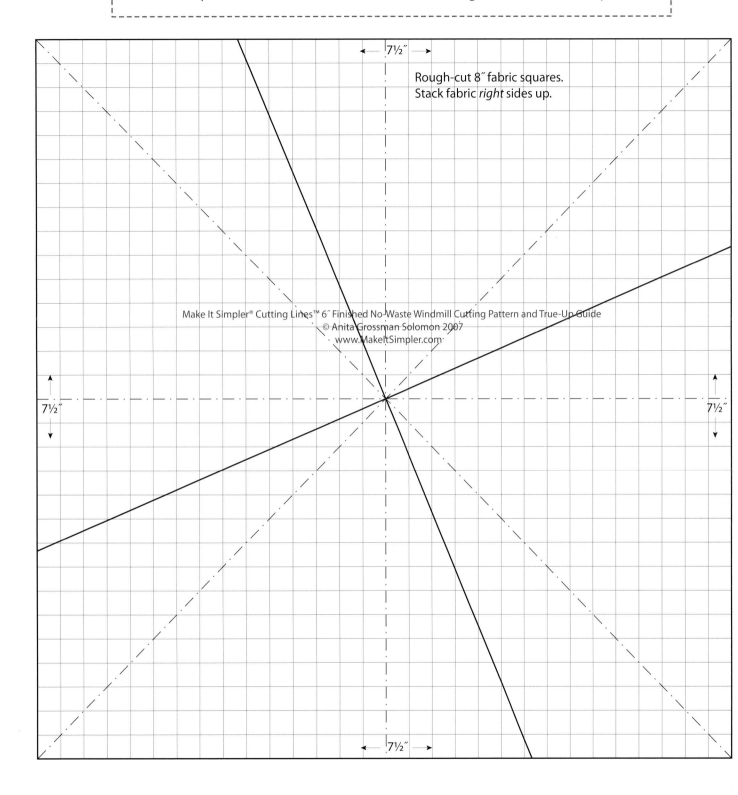

Rough-cut 8″ fabric squares.
Stack fabric *right* sides up.

7½″

7½″

7½″

7½″

Make It Simpler® Cutting Lines™ 6″ Finished No-Waste Windmill Cutting Pattern and True-Up Guide
© Anita Grossman Solomon 2007
www.MakeItSimpler.com

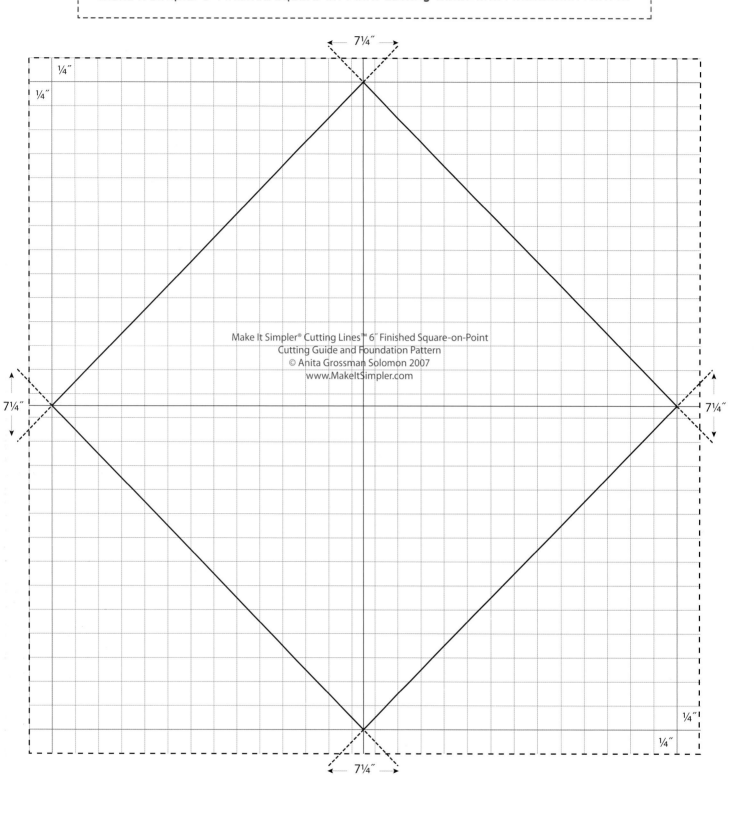

Make It Simpler® Cutting Lines™ 6″ Finished Square-on-Point
Cutting Guide and Foundation Pattern
© Anita Grossman Solomon 2007
www.MakeItSimpler.com

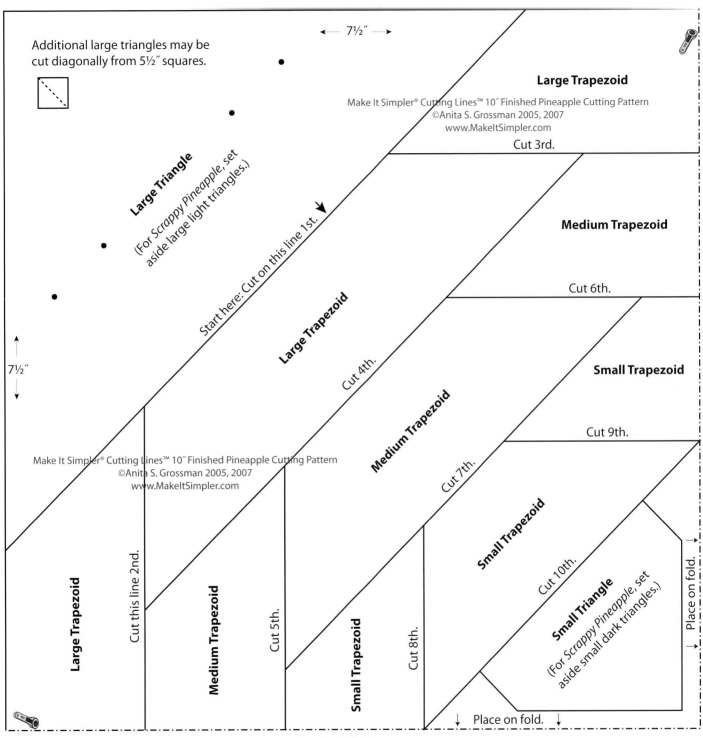

Additional large triangles may be cut diagonally from 5½″ squares.

7½″

Large Trapezoid

Make It Simpler® Cutting Lines™ 10″ Finished Pineapple Cutting Pattern
©Anita S. Grossman 2005, 2007
www.MakeItSimpler.com

Cut 3rd.

Large Triangle
(For *Scrappy Pineapple*, set aside large light triangles.)

Start here: Cut on this line 1st.

Medium Trapezoid

Cut 6th.

Large Trapezoid

Cut 4th.

Small Trapezoid

7½″

Cut 9th.

Medium Trapezoid

Make It Simpler® Cutting Lines™ 10″ Finished Pineapple Cutting Pattern
©Anita S. Grossman 2005, 2007
www.MakeItSimpler.com

Cut 7th.

Small Trapezoid

Cut 10th.

Small Triangle
(For *Scrappy Pineapple*, set aside small dark triangles.)

Large Trapezoid

Cut this line 2nd.

Medium Trapezoid

Cut 5th.

Small Trapezoid

Cut 8th.

Place on fold.

Place on fold.

Place on fold.

Trim away bottom and right margins (only) along both dashed lines.

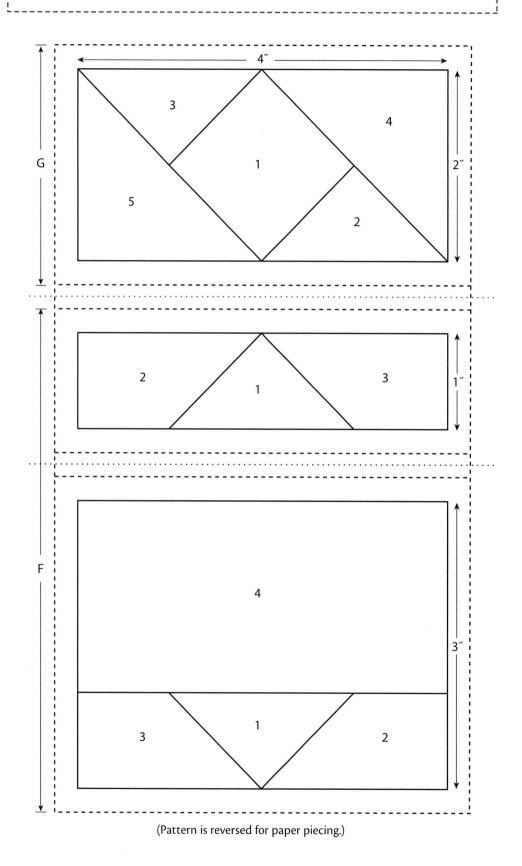

Make It Simpler Tropical Pineapple Border Foundation Piecing Pattern

(Pattern is reversed for paper piecing.)

(See schematic for piece placement on page 85.)

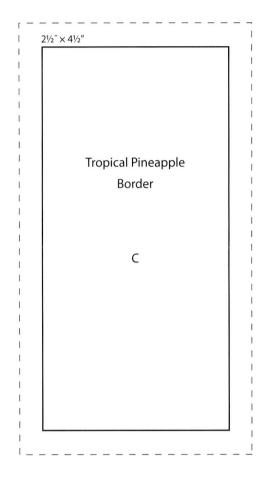

2½″ × 4½″

Tropical Pineapple
Border

C

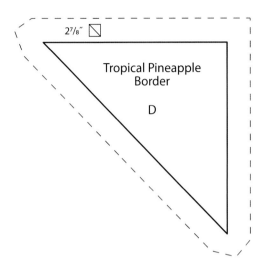

2⅞″

Tropical Pineapple
Border

D

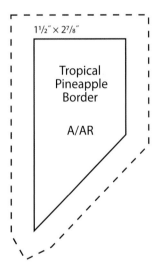

1½″ × 2⅞″

Tropical
Pineapple
Border

A/AR

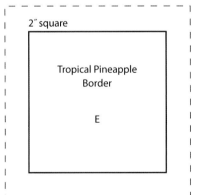

2″ square

Tropical Pineapple
Border

E

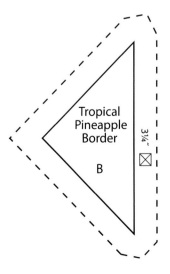

Tropical
Pineapple
Border

B

3¼″

(Sizes shown are for cut pieces.)

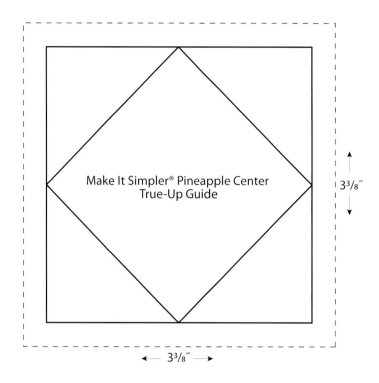

Make It Simpler® Pineapple Center
True-Up Guide

3³/₈″

3³/₈″

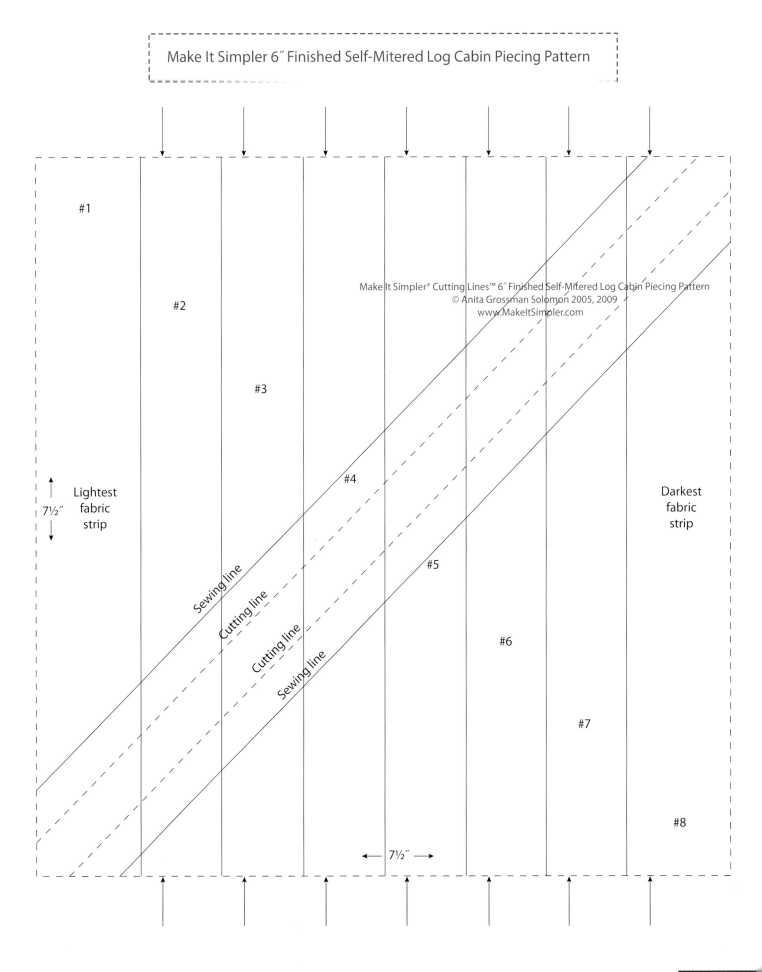

Make It Simpler 6″ Finished Self-Mitered Log Cabin Piecing Pattern

#1

#2

#3

#4

#5

#6

#7

#8

Make It Simpler® Cutting Lines™ 6″ Finished Self-Mitered Log Cabin Piecing Pattern
© Anita Grossman Solomon 2005, 2009
www.MakeItSimpler.com

Lightest fabric strip

7½″

Darkest fabric strip

Sewing line

Cutting line

Cutting line

Sewing line

7½″

Make It Simpler Block Cutting Chart

BLOCK	PAGE	FINISHED BLOCK SIZE	QUILT BLOCK	STEP 1: ROUGH-CUT SQUARE	STEP 2: TRIM SIZE (EXACT)	UNFINISHED BLOCK SIZE	CUTTING PATTERN	PIECING PATTERN	TRIMMING GUIDE
	21	9" square	No Patience Cut-As You-Go	7½"	7" square; 2" wide strip	9½" square	No	No	
	23	9" square	No Patience Square Cut	12"	11" square	9½" square	No	No	page 98
	27	15" square	No Patience Super-Sized	18"	8½" square (folded); 17" square (unfolded)	15½" square	No	No	
	31	7" square (1 unit); 14" square (four-patch square unit)	Xcentric	—	8½" square cut from unlaundered, unstarched yardage	7½" square (1 unit); 14½" square (Four-Patch square unit)	No	No	
	37	Various	Xcentric Super-Sized	Determined by choice of yardage			No	No	
	43	8½" square	Anita's Arrowhead	8½"	2 different 8" fabric squares	9" square (2 squares 8" trim make 1 block)	No	No	page 100
	49	6" square	Old Italian Block	8½"	8" square	6½" square	No	No	page 99
	55	6" square	No-Waste Windmill	8"	7½" square	6½" square	page 101	No	
	66	6" square	Square-on-Point	7¾"	7¼" square	6½" square	page 102	Optional page 102	
	73	10" square	Two-Color Pineapple	16"	7½" square (folded); 15" square (unfolded)	10½" square; 10½" × 5½" unfinished half-blocks		Optional	
	83	10" square	Scrappy Pineapple	16"	7½" square (folded); 15" square (unfolded)	10½" square	page 103	page 106	Make It Simpler Pineapple Trimming Guide (page 80)
	85	10" square	Tropical Pineapple	16"	7½" square (folded); 15" square (unfolded)	10½" square		Optional; yes for border page 104	
	88	6"	Self-Mitered Log Cabin		8" × 1½" strips	6½"	No	page 107	

Make It Simpler Supply List Chart

SUPPLIES, NONFABRIC		NO PATIENCE			XCENTRIC		ANITA'S ARROW-HEAD	OLD ITALIAN BLOCK	NO-WASTE WINDMILL	SQUARE-ON-POINT	PINEAPPLES			SELF-MITERED LOG CABIN
		Cut-As-You-Go	Square Cut	Super-Sized	Xcentric	Super-Sized					Scrappy	Two-Color	Tropical Border	
Square Rulers*	2½"										•	•	•	
	4½"										•	•		
	6½"	6½" square used for alternate block						•		•	•	•	•	•
	8"						•	•	•					•
	8½"			•	•									
	9½"		•					•						
	10"	When available												
	10½"										•	•		
	11"		•											
Rectangular Rulers*	3½" wide							•						
	Medium length	•	•		•			•	•	•	•	•	•	•
	Long			At least 16" long	15" square or larger for four-block unit	Yardstick and largest ruler available								

Ruler Notes: Manufacturers will introduce and discontinue rulers. Not every size listed may be available. In lieu of the above handy rulers, one 12½" square ruler would be adequate.

		Cut-As-You-Go	Square Cut	Super-Sized	Xcentric	Super-Sized	Anita's	Old Italian	No-Waste	Square-On-Point	Scrappy	Two-Color	Tropical Border	Self-Mitered
Marker	Washable marker or chalk pencil for rotary mat								•					
	Permanent medium-point or chalk pencil visible on fabric				•	•								
Marker; rubbing alcohol or nail polish remover	Permanent medium-point to mark guidelines on ruler	Optional			•	•	•	•	•	•				
Patterns		page 98					page 100	page 99	page 101	page 102	pages 103–106	pages 103–105		page 107
Paper	Simple Foundations Translucent Vellum							Optional, with Make It Simpler paper piecing		Optional, to isolate motif in square			•	•
	Parchment paper										•	•	•	
	Freezer paper, preferably 18" wide										•	•	•	
	Sticky notes 2" or 1⅞" wide						•		Optional					
Gluestick	Collins Fabric Gluestick or 3M Restickable							If paper pieced		•	•	•	•	•
Miscellaneous	Fusible non-woven interfacing										•	•		
General supplies	Scissors, seam ripper, straight pins, chalk, washable marker, permanent marker, alcohol, regular spray starch, design wall, sewing machine, surge protector, rotary cutter, and mat. (Old Italian Block cut on point requires minimum 11" × 11" mat.)													

INDEX

TIPS

ABOUT THE AUTHOR

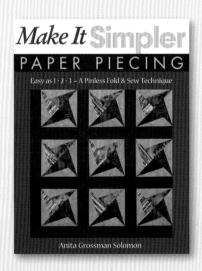

Anita Grossman Solomon is an award-winning quilter with a degree in art. Her inventive Make It Simpler methods make quiltmaking faster and easier. She pioneered Pinless Fold & Sew paper piecing and has now upended rotary cutting. With a fine arts background and interest in quilt history, her predilection is for artful scrap quilts. She lives and maintains her studio in midtown Manhattan.

Author's website: www.makeitsimpler.com

Fabric kits for *Rotary Cutting Revolution:*
www.cottonclub.com
The Cotton Club
P.O. Box 2263
Boise, ID 83701
208-345-5567

Also by Anita Grossman Solomon:

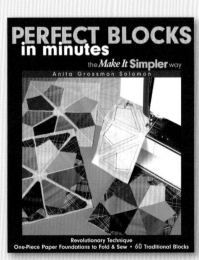

Great Titles *from* C&T PUBLISHING

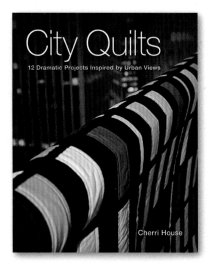

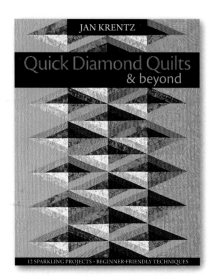

Available at your local retailer or **www.ctpub.com** *or* **800-284-1114**

For a list of other fine books from C&T Publishing, ask for a free catalog:

C&T PUBLISHING, INC.
P.O. Box 1456
Lafayette, CA 94549
800-284-1114

Email: ctinfo@ctpub.com
Website: www.ctpub.com

C&T Publishing's professional photography services are now available to the public. Visit us at www.ctmediaservices.com.

Tips and Techniques *can be found at www.ctpub.com > Consumer Resources > Quiltmaking Basics: Tips & Techniques for Quiltmaking & More*

For quilting supplies:

COTTON PATCH
1025 Brown Ave.
Lafayette, CA 94549
Store: 925-284-1177
Mail order: 925-283-7883

Email: CottonPa@aol.com
Website: www.quiltusa.com

Note: Fabrics used in the quilts shown may not be currently available, as fabric manufacturers keep most fabrics in print for only a short time.